Introduction

Each of us has many special memories. Some of these memories we recall almost every day. Other memories surface from time to time and provide a pleasant recollection. Every once in awhile I think of a friend I had in college and the good times we had trying to work our way through school. When I remember this friend, I always think of the time John F. Kennedy visited the campus at Southern Illinois University. I will always smile as I think of how we shoved and wormed our way through the throng to get a glimpse of him and Jackie. She had the biggest smile. It seemed to ignite the entire crowd. This moment of reminiscing also triggers sadder memories—the assassination of President Kennedy, the television coverage of the event, Jack Ruby's shooting of Lee Harvey Oswald, and most recently the death of Jacqueline Kennedy Onassis.

As we get older, the number of memories we have increases. This is only natural because a senior citizen has lived fifty or sixty years more than a recent college graduate and has had many more experiences. Each experience a person has creates memories—good, bad, or indifferent. It is hard to imagine just how many memories would be stored in the mind of a seventy-five year old grandfather or grandmother. So, here is a thought to ponder for a minute or two. Are memories forgotten? If a memory is forgotten, is it still a memory? Probably not, but it could still be on file somewhere in the deepest, darkest recesses of a person's mind. Perhaps it is simply in storage waiting for some stimuli to activate it.

A couple of weeks ago, while making a two-hour drive to my opthamologist, I was listening to the radio. A disc jockey played a "golden oldie." It was called "Crystal Blue Persuasion." I recognized the melody immediately and named the tune after just a few notes. I had forgotten all about this one-time favorite song that I had not heard for years. Was it a memory before I heard it that day or just a fact on file? After another few notes I remembered that a group named Tommy James and The Shondells had recorded this tune and made it popular.

It was then that my memory failed me. I could not remember the year the song was popular. But, in a moment or two, I recalled that "Crystal Blue Persuasion" was popular the July we took a family vacation to the Wisconsin Dells. Our son was three years old, and he loved going to a small amusement park and riding on a flying elephant. Since our son was born in 1966, it must have been 1969 when Tommy James and his cohorts rose to the top of the pop music charts.

Yes, the song triggered many memories of that summer and that vacation—some with great detail. I remembered that every news report contained updates about Teddy Kennedy and the incident at Chappaquidick. The name Mary Jo Kopechne came to my mind. I remembered how huge the mosquitoes can be that time of year in central Wisconsin. I remembered a restaurant at The Dells that served meals family style.

We hope that our daily presentations provide you with hours of reflection, remembering, and memory sharing. What were you doing in mid-July of 1969 when "Crystal Blue Persuasion" or some other tune was heard for the first time? Where did your family vacation when your first child was three years old? What were you doing the day President Kennedy was shot?

Just think of all the places you have traveled, be they near or far. Just think of all the people who have been a part of your life. Just think of the thousands of experiences you have had. Just think of the multitude of events that have taken place during your lifetime. It is impossible to remember everything. We hope this book will assist you in remembering many of your experiences.

To the Individual

Daily Doses of Nostalgia was created to help you recall the happenings, occurrences, and events of your life. The pictures and the daily presentations of events, past and present, were designed to act as catalysts for your memory. Each day you will read about an historical happening, an unusual event or the life of a famous or infamous person. Reading about the topic of the day is just the beginning and should take only a few minutes. But, hopefully, many stored memories will be awakened—memories that you associate with that event, person, or issue. Maybe a chain reaction will occur—one memory opening the window to another one long forgotten. Sharing these memories with a spouse, friend, or neighbor, when possible, can make each day just a little more interesting and fulfilling. And thinking about the answers to the questions following the main writeup will further enhance the remembering process.

To the Activity Professional
Using the Illustrations

Sometimes a picture can be worth a thousand words. It is hoped that the illustrations in this book trigger a thousand memories. On some days the illustration alone may be used to jog memories. You could make a copy of the illustration for each person in your group, or you could mount a copy on a sheet of construction paper and pass it around or place it on a small easel. Or, simply hold up the book for all to see. Place a paper clip on the page so it can easily be found if the page is lost. Some of the illustrations have been specifically created for participants who enjoy coloring.

While the participants are viewing a picture or passing it around, ask introductory questions such as the following: What is the date today? What day of the week is it? Does anything about the illustration seem familiar? What do you think we will be remembering and talking about today? What is special about today?

Presenting the Information

The text for each day offers interesting and valuable information concerning the occurrence on that date. Before each session, read the information a couple of times to familiarize yourself. Use a marker to highlight important points you want to relate. Try not to read the information word-for-word. Present it as a conversation, a story hour. Do not relate too many details such as dates, foreign names, and numbers. Too much of this is boring and confusing and detracts from the basic concepts. A casual approach will put the participants at ease.

Questions and/or statements follow the basic information. These are designed to encourage participation and the sharing of insights, opinions, and memories. Here are some points to consider during the preparation and presentation of the session:

1. You do not have to use all the questions. Look them over. Decide which ones will motivate your group, and solicit participation.
2. Don't force someone to participate. Encourage, but don't force. Some memories can be too personal to share.
3. When discussion slows, ask another question.
4. Don't allow one or two people to dominate. Encourage others to enter by asking, "Does anyone else have a special memory, or do you agree?"
5. The content of the text may help you to think of questions of your own. GREAT! You may know specific facts about the topic or about a member of your group. (Mrs. Kamenski lived most of her life in New York, and today's focus is the Empire State Building.)
6. Keep the length of a session to around half an hour. Short and interesting is better than long and boring. Let interest and participation guide the length.
7. Don't use this book every day as a group activity. It would soon lose its appeal. For a change, duplicate and place copies of the day's event on a bulletin board. Occasionally deliver copies to the rooms of those interested. They can read on their own and come to a discussion session later in the day. Or, place the copies at the appropriate lunch settings.
8. The picture and text can be used with individuals (one-on-one), as well as with groups. Make the material available to staff members. It can be a topic of conversation while the room is being cleaned, while the bed is being made, while the client is being dressed, etc. A staff member could say, "Did you know today was Gary Cooper's birthday? Did you ever see a Gary Cooper movie such as *Sergeant York* or *Friendly Persuasion*? Do you think he was a good actor?"
9. If you have retired schoolteachers who do volunteer work at your facility, they might enjoy leading a discussion group.

Daily Doses of Nostalgia
September

Table of Contents

September 1

September	1	National Better Breakfast Month	4
September	2	George Bush Parachuted from Plane	6
September	3	Labor Day	8
September	4	Paul Harvey Born	10
September	5	Cassius Clay Knocks Out Petrzykowski	12
September	6	Jane Addams Born	14
September	7	Grandma Moses Born	16
September	8	St. Augustine Founded	17
September	9	Birthday of Colonel Sanders	20
September	10	Invention of the Sewing Machine	22
September	11	TV's Fall Flops and Boring Celebrities	24
September	12	Jesse Owens Born	26
September	13	National Grandparents' Day	28
September	14	"The Star-Spangled Banner" Was Written	30
September	15	National Hispanic Heritage Month	32
September	16	*Mayflower* Sailed for Virginia	34
September	17	Citizenship Day	36
September	18	Horse Outran Locomotive	38
September	19	Gettysburg Address	40
September	20	Jackson County Apple Festival	42
September	21	The First Day of Autumn	44
September	22	Ice Cream Cone Created	46
September	23	Birthday of Mickey Rooney	48
September	24	National Dog Week	50
September	25	Great American Dulcimer Convention	52
September	26	Birth of George Gershwin	54
September	27	American Indian Day	56
September	28	State Fair of Texas	58
September	29	Oktoberfest at the Amana Colonies	60
September	30	Babe Ruth Hit His 60th Home Run	62

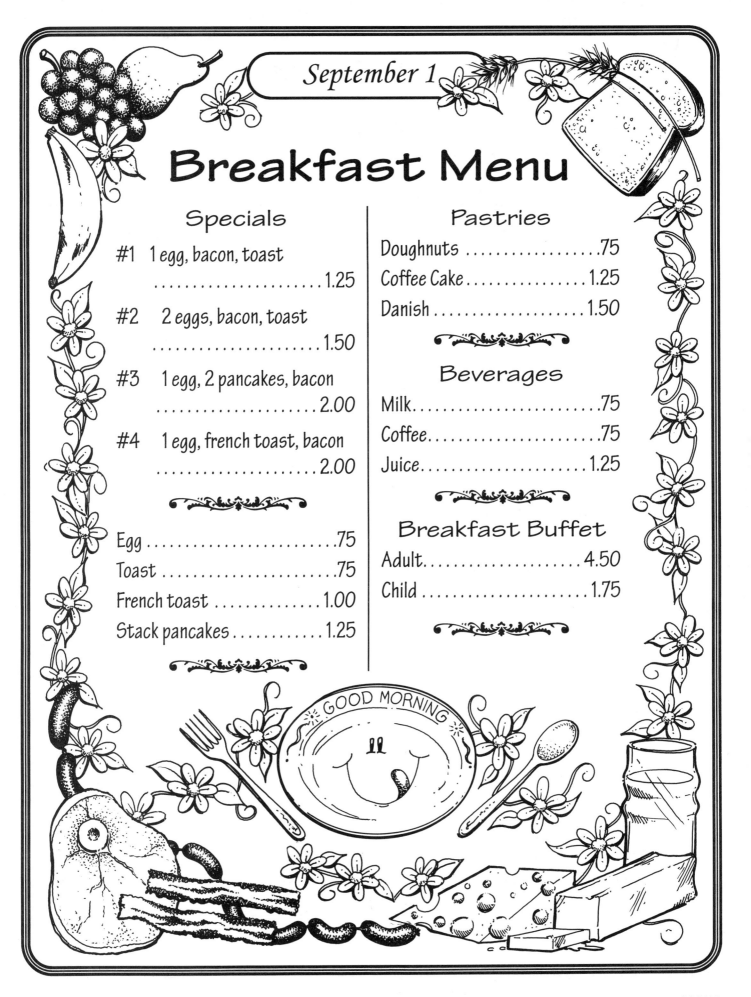

September 1

Breakfast Menu

Specials

#1 1 egg, bacon, toast 1.25

#2 2 eggs, bacon, toast 1.50

#3 1 egg, 2 pancakes, bacon 2.00

#4 1 egg, french toast, bacon 2.00

Egg 75
Toast 75
French toast 1.00
Stack pancakes 1.25

Pastries

Doughnuts 75
Coffee Cake 1.25
Danish 1.50

Beverages

Milk........................75
Coffee.....................75
Juice.....................1.25

Breakfast Buffet

Adult.....................4.50
Child.....................1.75

It happens the entire month of September.

National Better Breakfast Month

Starting on the first, the entire month of September is National Better Breakfast Month. The idea of good nutrition is very important. It's true that a lot of people don't eat breakfast, or they only grab one item, such as a roll, while they are on the run. But, most doctors and nutritionists consider breakfast to be the most important meal of the day. They state that you should eat a good breakfast at the same time every day. This will give your biochemical clock a starting point. Your adrenal hormones are at their best each morning when you arise. This is why you should start your day with fresh fruit, meat, whole grain bread and cereal, butter, and eggs. Stick with the four basic food groups of fruits and vegetables, breads and cereals, meats, and dairy.

1. Do you remember when milk was delivered by a milkman to your home?
2. What time did you have to get up for breakfast when you were young?
3. Did you have chores to do before or after breakfast? What types of chores did you have to do?
4. What kind of meat did you usually have for breakfast? Do you remember where the meat came from? Was it bought in a store or brought in from a smokehouse?
5. How about eggs? Did your parents have their own chickens? What kind of food did you have to feed them? Did you help gather the eggs? How many times a day?
6. What is your favorite breakfast food?
7. Which juice do you like best—orange, pineapple, grapefruit, apple, prune, cranberry? Why?
8. Can you share with us a time when you ate something silly (like cold pizza) for breakfast?
9. Share with us a memory from when you cooked breakfast for your family.

Activity

1. Provide variety-pack-sized boxes of cereals for each participant. Lead an examination of the boxes to discover the sugar content, food value, etc., of each type. Have a taste test. Provide samples of five different cereals for each person to taste. Allow time for each person to tell the group which is his/her favorite and why.
2. Select several different cereals from the grocer's shelf. Make your selection as varied as possible. After discussing the design of each box for eye appeal and taste promises, place a sample of each in small baggies for each person to taste. After the tasting, discuss the difference between the advertising promise and the real taste.

It happened on September 2, 1944.

George Bush Parachuted from Plane

On September 2, 1944, during World War II, pilot George Bush was shot down in the South Pacific by the Japanese. He was rescued and picked up by the American submarine *Finback,* but his two crew members were killed.

This is an interesting event because it concerns the fate of our future forty-first President. But, it is also interesting for another reason. When Bush jumped out of his burning airplane, the parachute that saved him was composed of webbing made from U.S.-grown hemp (Cannabis sativa).

Hemp has been used as a fabric and textile for a long time in the United States. The first two copies of the Declaration of Independence were written on Dutch hemp paper. Benjamin Franklin started one of our first paper mills that used cannabis. And, in 1850 a U.S. census report stated that 8,327 hemp plantations were in the United States.

Up until around 1820 about eighty percent of all fabrics and textiles used for bed sheets, towels, clothes, tents, rugs, flags, and other items were made mainly from hemp fibers.

After this time the United States put restrictions on the cultivation of hemp, and we looked for other materials to use in textiles and fabrics. However, during World War II our Agriculture Department urged farmers to grow hemp for use during wartime. And, in 1943 the University of Kentucky Agricultural Extension Service asked its 4-H clubs to grow hemp for fiber to help their country in wartime.

When the war ended, hemp went out of style again because of the effects of smoking cannabis. Today, hemp as a fabric is making an amazing comeback. In stores throughout the United States, a person can purchase pants, shirts, blouses, purses, knapsacks, and even necklaces made of hemp.

1. Did you belong to a 4-H club during World War II that was asked to grow hemp in order to aid your country during wartime?
2. Is there any clothing that you wear today made from hemp?
3. Was your home state one of the regions in which hemp was grown?

Activity

Make a list of other fabrics used in the United States. Also, show different samples of several fabrics, allowing group members to touch them.

It happens around September 3.

Labor Day

Labor Day is a holiday honoring working people. It is a legal holiday held on the first Monday in September and is observed on this day in all states, Puerto Rico, and Canada. It is a day of recreation and rest.

Two people are credited with the founding of this holiday. They are Peter J. McGuire, a carpenter from New York, who helped create the United Brotherhood of Carpenters and Joiners; and Matthew Maquire, a machinist, who lived in Patterson, New Jersey. Both of these were leaders in organizing the first Labor Day parade in New York City on September 5, 1882. A union resolution in 1883 declared the first Monday in September each year as Labor Day. More than half the states were observing Labor Day on one day or another by 1893 when a bill was introduced in Congress to establish Labor Day as a federal holiday. President Grover Cleveland signed into law an act making the first Monday in September a legal holiday for federal employees and the District of Columbia. This was on June 28, 1894. The first Labor Day celebrated as a legal public holiday was on September 3, 1894.

Labor is a human activity that provides the services or goods in an economy. So, it is appropriate that we have a special day honoring the working men and women of this country.

1. Many cities have Labor Day parades. Macy's Department Store sponsors a Thanksgiving Day parade. What other holidays and special days include a parade?

St. Patrick's Day	Rose Bowl
Santa's arrival	Miss America Pageant
Mardi Gras	100 or 150 year celebration
Fourth of July	the founding of a community
Political convention	Protest/demonstration

2. Share with us a time when you paraded. What was the occasion? What did you wear? Did you walk, ride a float, or ride a horse?
3. Who (what occupations) has to work on Labor Day?
4. Do you remember your first job? How did you get it, and what did you have to do at your job?
5. What occupation(s) have you had as an adult? Did you enjoy your work?

Activity

A few people might pantomime different jobs. Others can guess what these jobs are. Or, you can make a list of jobs "A to Z." Start by listing jobs members of the group formed.

It happened on September 4, 1918.

Paul Harvey Born

Paul Harvey, the famous news commentator, columnist, and author, was born in Tulsa, Oklahoma, on September 4, 1918. One of his first jobs was as a radio announcer at station KVOO in Tulsa. Following this, he held a succession of jobs, including station manager and program director in Kansas, Michigan, and Missouri.

In 1944 he was a news commentator and analyst for ABC. He became very popular as a commentator, then as a syndicated columnist for the *Los Angeles Times* in 1954. In 1968 he began a career as a TV commentator. While doing all of this, he still continued his daily radio show.

His "The Rest of the Story" became a popular feature on his radio show, and thousands of listeners across the United States turned to his program daily. *The Rest of the Story* was published as a novel in 1956. He also wrote *Remember These Things* (1952), *Autumn of Liberty* (1954), and *You Said It, Paul Harvey* (1969).

Harvey has been honored with every journalism and humanitarian award possible. The Veterans of Foreign Wars, American Legion, Freedom Foundation, Radio Broadcasters Association, American Academy of Family Physicians, International Radio and TV Society, and the Salvation Army are just a few of the organizations who have bestowed honors upon him. All of these awards culminated with his induction in the Emerson Radio Hall of Fame in 1990.

1. Did you ever listen to Paul Harvey on the radio or see him on television? Did you enjoy his radio programs? At different times his programs were controversial. Did you agree or disagree with his opinions?
2. "The Rest of the Story" was always in two parts. Harvey told the first part of a story at the beginning of a program and the rest of it towards the program's end. Many listeners can still recall favorite stories he told. Do you remember a particular story of his?
3. Did you ever read any of Paul Harvey's novels? Which ones? Can you tell a little bit about one of them?
4. What about Paul Harvey's personal life? Was he married? Did he have any children? From what city and state was his radio show broadcast?
5. Can you think of any other famous radio personalities? (Example: Walter Winchell)

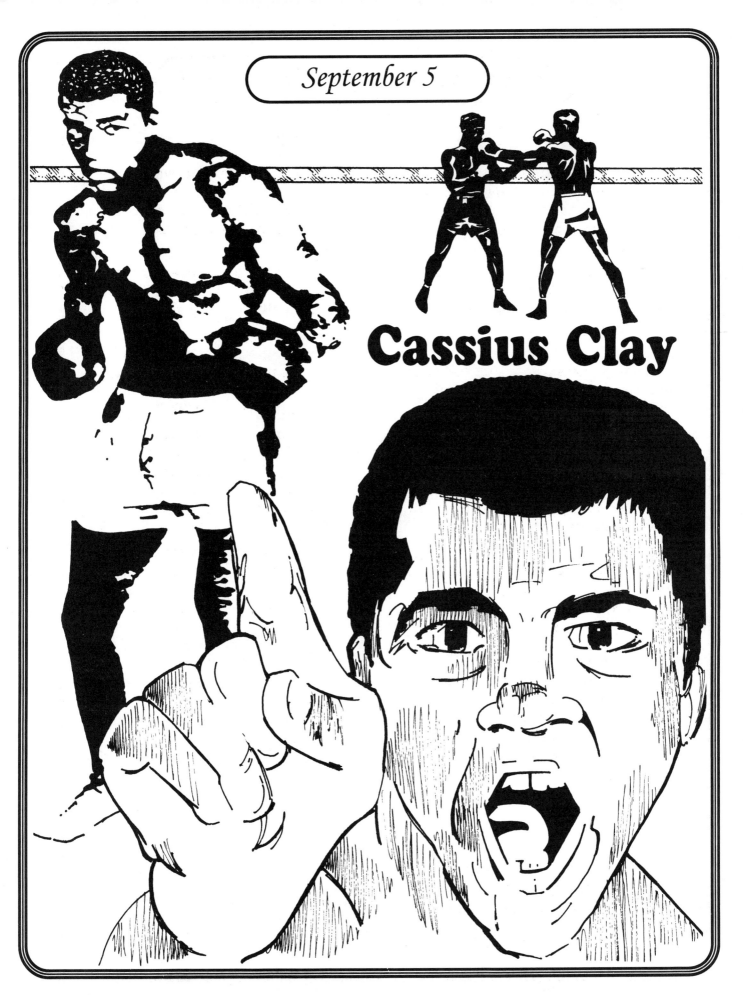

It happened on September 5, 1960.

Cassius Clay Knocks Out Pietrzykowski

On September 5, 1960, Cassius Marcellus Clay, Jr., scored a unanimous decision over Zbigniew Pietrzykowski in the light-heavyweight division and won an Olympic gold medal. This brought the unknown boxer to world attention.

He quickly rose to prominence after he won a surprising victory over the heavyweight champion Sonny Liston in 1964. From that time on, his name was constantly in the media.

Next, Clay won a championship bout from Liston to gain the heavyweight title, and he changed his name to Muhammad Ali. This was a result of his conversion to the Black Muslim religion.

His next fight with Liston was very controversial because Liston went down and stayed down in the first round. Ali, though, proved to be a champion who accepted all challenges and fought all heavyweights with ranking credentials.

He was stripped of his title in 1967 because he refused military service on religious grounds during the Vietnam War but was allowed to begin fighting again in 1970. He also had his appeal of conviction upheld by the U.S. Supreme Court in 1971. Ali regained the world championship in a bout in 1974 with George Foreman. He lost his crown again in 1978 to Leon Spinks but won it back the same year and became the first man to win the title three times.

The only boxers to defeat Ali, other than Spinks, were Joe Frazier in 1971, Ken Norton in 1973 (who later lost to Ali), Larry Holmes in 1980 (who stopped Ali's attempt at a a fourth heavyweight championship), and Trevor Berbick in 1981. After this fight Ali stated he was retiring. His record through 1982 was 55-5.

Muhammad Ali was perhaps the most celebrated sports figure in the world during the 1960s and 1970s. His vivacious personality, his role as a spokesman for black Americans, and his tremendous staying power as an athlete made him a dominant figure.

1. Muhammad Ali was idolized by many black Americans and by millions of people all over the world. There were comic books published that presented his boxing exploits and the good deeds he performed. Did you consider him to be an idol and a role model? How would you characterize him?
2. Were you ever at ringside during one of his bouts, or have you watched him fight on television? Describe his fighting style. (He was known for his precise punching and great speed. As his physical abilities lessened because of age, Ali used tactical skills to win.)
3. Ali had a tremendous personality and was quite a wit. Do you recall any time when he showed these qualities?
4. Here are sixteen sports figures who are/were good/bad role models: Pete Rose, Babe Ruth, Joe DiMagio, Arnold Palmer, Magic Johnson, Michael Jordan, Ted Williams, Joe Louis, O.J. Simpson, Greg Louganis, Chris Evert, Althea Gibson, Jackie Joyner-Kersee, Nancy Kerrigan, Tonya Harding, and Billie Jean King. Which of these are/were good role models? Why do you feel this way?

It happened on September 6, 1860.

Jane Addams Born

In the fall of 1889, pioneer social worker Jane Addams and her school friend Ellen Gates Starr settled in a broken-down old mansion near the West Side of Chicago. This was an area of sweatshops and tenements. The old mansion, Hull House, soon became the most well-known social settlement in this country.

At Hull House, Addams and her associates nursed the sick, fed the hungry, and helped wayward girls and boys. They worked to improve conditions in the sweatshops and demanded the city clean up the filthy streets. She was instrumental in establishing the first juvenile court in the country.

As the president of the Women's International League for Peace and Freedom, she fought for negotiations instead of war. She was awarded the Nobel Peace prize in 1931.

Jane Addams managed Hull House for forty-six years. During that time she became one of the most famous and most loved people in the United States.

Addams was born on September 6, 1860, in Cedarville, Illinois. As a young girl she saw how terribly poor people in the streets close to factories were, and she told her father that someday she would live next to poor people. She went to Europe in 1883. There she also saw hunger and terrible conditions in the large cities. She stayed for a time at Toynbee Hall in the city of London. This was the first-known social settlement. These experiences would lead her to establish Hull House in America.

1. As a child do you remember if there were homeless people? Did any hobos come to your family's door for food? What did your mother feed them? Did any of them do any chores such as chopping wood to earn their food?
2. What agencies exist to help the poor, hungry, and homeless in your community, in the United States, or in the world? Name some and share what they do. (Red Cross, YMCA, Salvation Army, etc.)
3. How has the homeless situation changed in the last twenty years?
4. How have you ever helped someone who was down on his/her luck?
5. Who are some other famous women? What have they contributed to our society? Discuss and make a complete study of this subject.

Activity

Share information with the group about an organization or agency in your community that may be unknown to them. (A halfway house, home for battered women, subsidized housing complex, etc.)

It happened on September 7, 1860.

Grandma Moses Born

Grandma Moses (Anna Mary Robertson) was born on September 7, 1860. Her birth and childhood took place on a farm in Greenwich, New York. She married Thomas Moses in 1887 and moved to a farm near Staunton, Virginia. In 1905 they returned to rural Eagle Bridge, New York, where the rest of her life was spent on the family farm.

She became America's most famous primitive painter. As a young lady, she embroidered pictures on canvas. But, as she grew older, arthritis made it difficult for her to use her hands in working with yarn. She began painting when she was seventy-six years old. Her gaily painted pictures were scenes well known to her. They were people working on the farm and children playing in a country scene–all filled with charm and innocence.

In the beginning she gave her paintings away. Then she sold some for little money. An art collector discovered her work in 1939. That same year she had a showing at the Museum of Modern Art in New York City. She soon became famous throughout the United States and much of the world.

She painted around two thousand paintings before her death in 1861 at 101 years of age. A lot of her paintings have been on holiday cards. "Out for the Christmas Trees," Over the River to Grandma's House," and "Sugaring Off" are three of her more famous works.

1. Do you recall the first time you saw any of Grandma Moses' paintings? How old were you? Was the painting on a greeting card?
2. Grandma Moses lived to be 101 years of age (1860 until 1961). Think of all of the events that took place during those years. Can you name several?
3. Who was your favorite grandmother? Why was she so special to you?
4. Where did your grandmother live? In town? In a rural setting?
5. What are some of the things you did at her house? How often did you get to see her?

Activity

Grandma Moses didn't draw any better than most people. Give each participant a sheet of paper and a colored marker. Ask each to draw a house or any scene they wish.

It happened on September 8, 1565.

St. Augustine Founded

The oldest permanent settlement in the United States is St. Augustine, Florida. It was founded on September 8, 1565, by Pedro Menendez de Aviles, a Spanish explorer.

St. Augustine was ruled by Spain for over 200 years. In the early years the town was attacked several times by the English. Sir Francis Drake looted and burned the settlement in 1586. Spain ceded Florida to Britain. Spain governed the settlement again from 1783 until 1821 when Florida became part of the United States.

St. Augustine is located in northeastern Florida on the Atlantic Ocean. The Spanish-style architecture and narrow streets exemplify the city's long and colorful past. Spanish houses, some newly restored, line the narrow streets. The Castillo de San Marcos, a large stone fortress built by the Spanish in the 1600s, lies just outside the old city gates.

Today, the most important industry of the city is tourism. Every year visitors come to St. Augustine for the climate, the beaches, and to learn of its history.

1. Have you ever been on vacation in Florida? What did you see? Did you go to Bush Gardens, Walt Disney World, or Cypress Gardens? Did any of your grandchildren go with you? What unusual sights did you see?
2. When you were young, what places did you and your parents visit in the United States?
3. What was the best vacation you ever had? Who went with you? What do you remember?
4. How many towns, rivers, and colleges begin with Saint? (St. Charles River; St. Clair River; Saint Augustine College; St. Charles, Illinois, etc.)
5. We have many words in our language borrowed from Spanish. *Lasso*, *stampede*, *corral*, *mesa*, *cinch*, *rodeo*, and *sombrero* are examples. In what part of the United States did these words originate? Why do you think this is so?
6. Which of our towns/cities have Spanish names? (Los Angeles, Amarillo, El Paso, San Diego, Phoenix, etc.)

It happened on September 9, 1890.

Birthday of Colonel Sanders

When we think of Colonel Harland Sanders, we think of "finger-lickin' good" *Kentucky Fried Chicken*™, and we picture the Colonel with white hair, moustache, goatee, shirt, suit, black string tie, black shoes, and a cane.

The honorary title was given to him by the Governor of Kentucky in 1936, but he wasn't born in Kentucky. He was born on September 9, 1890, near Henryville, Indiana. His family was very poor. And, as the oldest of three children, he cooked and cared for the other two. By the time he was seven, he was already a good cook.

The beginning of the seventh grade was the end of his formal education. From that time on, Harland had several different jobs and even spent a year in the army. In 1929 he had a filling station in Corbin, Kentucky. There he fed his family and travelers who stopped by. His southern fried chicken eventually made him famous, and he opened a large cafe.

He began having so many customers that he ran into a problem. Pan-frying was too slow. So, in 1939 he perfected a cooking method using a pressure cooker. He also experimented with herbs and spices and came up with the mix that is used by the franchises today.

In 1956 he had to sell his restaurant to pay his debts. He was sixty-six and almost broke. So he took to the road and began selling Kentucky Fried Chicken franchises. The rest is history. By 1964 he had more than six hundred franchises, and he sold his company to John Y. Brown, Jr., for $2,000,000 and $75,000 a year salary for publicity work. Brown, using the Colonel as an image, expanded until there were 3,500 franchises in 1971 at which time Kentucky Fried Chicken was bought by Heublein, Inc.

For years Colonel Sanders travelled around 200,000 miles annually to promote Kentucky Fried Chicken. He used his wealth to help churches, the Boy Scouts, the Salvation Army, and orphans.

1. Do you remember Sunday dinner at home or at your grandparents' house? Did you have chicken? What other dishes were served with it?
2. Did you or your family ever raise chickens? Whose job was it to take care of them? Describe the work required.
3. Colonel Sanders used herbs and spices to prepare his chicken. How many different ways have you prepared and eaten chicken?
4. Sanders used his wealth to help churches, the Boy Scouts, the Salvation Army, and orphans. Have you ever contributed to or worked for any of these charities?
5. Have you ever worked for a franchise or owned a franchise? What was the name of it, and what did your work entail?
6. Have you eaten Kentucky Fried Chicken? Which did you prefer—original or crispy? What side dishes are offered? Which do you like?

Activity

Now would be a good time to enjoy a chicken dinner. The facility's cook could come in to discuss the preparation of the meal. Or, why not order out and enjoy the Colonel's secret recipe.

It happened on September 10, 1846.

Invention of the Sewing Machine

The sewing machine, an invention that established mass production of sewn materials and played an important role in American industry during the 1800s, was patented by Elias Howe on September 10, 1846.

As a young man, Howe worked in Boston as a machinist. A few years later he discovered there was a need for a sewing machine, and he undertook the task of building one. He had many problems with his machine, and he had very little money. He even had to move his family into his father's house. But he persisted, and in 1845 he completed a machine that sewed 250 stitches a minute. Until that time the fastest a woman could sew by hand was about fifty stitches a minute.

He couldn't find a market for his machine in America. People in the garment industry were worried the machine would put them out of work, so they refused to buy it.

Howe went to England and sold the rights to his machine. While he was there, several American manufacturers, such as Isaac Singer, started making sewing machines. Howe brought suit against them, and in 1854 the courts ruled he had the right to collect royalties on all sewing machines made. In a few short years the sales of sewing machines made Howe $200,000 a year.

1. Do you remember if your mother sewed? Did she own a sewing machine? What brand was it?
2. If she sewed, what items did she make? Discuss what you remember.
3. Were you a seamstress as a child or as an adult? How did you begin? Who taught you? How long have you sewn? Have you ever sold any items you made?
4. What types of fabrics and materials did you like to work with?
5. What sort of attachments fit on your machine? (Buttonholer, etc.)
6. Was your sewing machine a portable, or was it in a sewing cabinet?
7. What other inventions have made our lives easier in modern times? (Air-conditioning, light bulb, automobile, vacuum cleaner, power lawn mower, etc.)

Activity

Have each person write down what he/she thinks the three greatest inventions have been. Tally the results and put in order from 1-10. Then, discuss what inventions are missing and whether the ranking should be changed.

September 11

Boring Institute

Boring Boring Boring
Boring Boring Boring
Boring Boring Boring
Boring Boring Boring
Boring Boring Boring
Boring Boring Boring
Boring Boring Boring
Boring Boring Boring
Boring Boring Boring
Boring Boring Boring
Boring Boring Boring
Boring Boring Boring

TV's Fall Flops

It happened around September 11.

TV's Fall Flops and Boring Celebrities

Each year, at this time in September, The Boring Institute issues its "Fearless Forecasts of TV's Fall Flops" and announces its annual "Most Boring Celebrities of the Year."

For the TV forecast of 1994, the Institute made the following statement. "It's the bland leading the bland. Despite the usual hype, there will be no hits among the nearly thirty, demographically dippy, new shows being introduced and most will have mercifully short lives in one of the worst new television seasons ever for the networks."

Concerning celebrities of 1994 who had massive media overexposure, the Institute listed O.J. Simpson, Paula Jones, Prince Charles, Roseanne and Tom Arnold, Bob Barker, Michael Fay, Michael Jackson and Lisa Marie Presley, Garth Brooks, Kurt Cobain, and the people from Arkansas.

Founded in 1984 by Alan Caruba, the Boring Institute has become one of the most popular media spoofs in the United States. (It has also become one of the most accurate in forecasting television flops.) "We try to get a good cross-section when we select our favorite boring celebrities by year's end, but this year, for example, there are no sports bores because it seemed like most sports got cancelled for some reason," stated Caruba.

1. What are the five worst TV shows you have seen?
2. Name the most terrible television show or series you have ever witnessed. Who was in it? What was it about? What year was it on? How long did it last?
3. Why do we seem to have so many really bad shows on television?
4. List several celebrities whom you are absolutely bored with seeing or hearing about.
5. Why does the media put so much exposure on one person?
6. Are you ever bored? What bores you? How do you break your boredom? (If you wish a copy of "TV's Flops and Most Boring Celebrities," write to Alan Caruba, The Boring Institute, Box 40, Maplewood, NJ 07040.)

Activity

Here is a "match" list for you to make copies of and give to the group for their enjoyment. They are to match the show to its sponsor.

1. Chrysler — Red Skelton
2. Jell-O — Sky King
3. Ovaltine — Ozzie and Harriet
4. Johnson's Wax — Milton Berle
5. Sealtest — Bob Hope
6. Nabisco — College Bowl
7. Carnation — Jet Jackson
8. Texaco — Perry Como
9. General Electric — Bat Masterson
10. Kraft — Jack Benny

Answers:
1. Bob Hope
2. Jack Benny
3. Jet Jackson
4. Red Skelton
5. Bat Masterson
6. Sky King
7. Ozzie and Harriet
8. Milton Berle
9. College Bowl
10. Perry Como

It happened on September 12, 1913.

Jesse Owens Born

James Cleveland Owens, better known as Jesse Owens, was born in Oakville, Alabama, on September 12, 1913. His father was a sharecropper. Later, the family moved to Cleveland, Ohio. Owens attended Ohio State University where he was a track and field star. In 1935 he broke three world records and tied a fourth.

But, it was his achievements at the 1936 Summer Olympic Games in Berlin that made him a sports legend. At these games he won four gold medals. He was a member of the U.S. 400-meter relay team that won, and he individually won the 100-meter race, the 200-meter race, and the broad jump.

Owens was black, and his performances enraged Adolf Hitler and other members of the Nazi Party. They had believed their Aryan white race would dominate the games. Nazi Party propaganda stated the white race was supreme. Owens proved them wrong.

Jesse believed that on the playing field all people are equal. In his later community service he travelled all over the country and gave speeches that promoted patriotism, clean living, and fair play.

1. As a youngster, what games did you play? Did you ever play marbles or hopscotch? What were some other games you remember playing?
2. What was your favorite participation sport? Why did you enjoy it?
3. Were any of your children involved in sports? What was the sport, and how long did they play?
4. Has there been a college or professional athlete in your family? Who was it, and what sport did he/she participate in?
5. Have you or any other family member been an Olympic athlete?
6. Have you ever attended any Olympic games? What year did you go, and what events did you observe?
7. Have you ever seen Jesse Owens winning an event during the 1936 Olympic Games either on TV or in a movie short?
8. What sport do you enjoy watching today? How often do you watch it? Do you have a favorite team?
9. As a black American, Jesse Owens suffered prejudice from the Nazis at the Olympic games. Were you ever a victim of prejudice? Why? When? Where? In addition to color, what are other prejudices that people have? When does jealousy become prejudice?

Activity

Devise a variety of 100-meter races for the participants. Outside or in a corridor measure 100 meters. Then, your group can participate in the following:

A. Carrying a potato on a spoon
B. Kicking a paperwad the size of a softball from one end to the other
C. Carrying two plastic bowling pins from one end to the other
D. Pushing a rolling chair in front of him/her
E. Walking to the opposite end with gloves on, then unwrapping a stick of gum, putting it into his/her mouth, and returning to the starting point

It happens the first Sunday after Labor Day.

National Grandparents' Day

The first Sunday after Labor Day is National Grandparents' Day. This is a special day for us to honor our grandparents and to help children become aware of the guidance and information older people are able to give.

In many countries, such as India and Nepal, the older members of a family are honored for their wisdom and highly respected by everyone in the community. In cultures like these, the older people play important roles in bringing up the children.

People are living longer today. Years ago the average life span was about forty-eight years. In the 1980s, life expectancy was estimated in the seventies. Today it is even higher, and a larger amount of people are living longer every year.

Many grandparents live in their own homes, in retirement communities, or nursing homes. Some, especially in rural areas, live with their families. These people, whether they live far or near, are very important to their families and should be especially remembered each year on their own important day.

1. Can you recall visits you made to the homes of your grandparents? What do you remember?
2. Are any of you grandparents? How many grandchildren do you have? What are their names? What are their ages?
3. Do any of you have great grandchildren?
4. What do you enjoy about being a grandparent?
5. How much time do you and your grandchildren spend together?
6. Are grandchildren of today as respectful as when you were a child?

Activity

Each person can make a list that presents information on the name, age, and activities of each grandchild. These lists can be placed on a bulletin board along with pictures of the children.

It happened on September 14, 1814.

"*The Star-Spangled Banner*" *Was Written*

"The Star-Spangled Banner" was written on September 14, 1814, by Francis Scott Key. On this day he was aboard a prisoner-exchange ship in Baltimore Harbor. From there, he witnessed the British fleet bombarding Fort McHenry throughout the night.

The next day he looked and saw that "our flag was still there." He was so inspired by the sight that he wrote a poem about it. The music for our anthem Key took from an English drinking song "To Anacreon in Heaven." Congress made "The Star-Spangled Banner" our national anthem in 1931.

Key had been on board the prisoner-exchange ship trying to get his friend William Beanes released from the British. When the British had left Washington in retreat during the War of 1812, they had taken Beanes with them. Key had received permission from President James Madison to intercede with the British for Beanes' release.

Key was a Washington lawyer and verse writer. Much of his poetry was religious.

1. Did you and your fellow students say the "Pledge of Allegiance" in grade school or high school? Let's say it once again.
2. What patriotic songs did you learn as a child, and in what events did you sing them? Were you in any patriotic parades?
3. Were any members of your family in the service during World War II or the Korean War?
4. Did you serve? If so, in what branch and in what part of the world?
5. What does our flag mean to you as an individual?
6. For several years there has been some talk of selecting a different national anthem. What do you think? Should we change our national anthem? Do you have a suggestion for a new anthem? Why do some people want the national anthem changed?

Activity

Do all the people know the words to "The Star-Spangled Banner"? Have each participant attempt to write the words on a piece of paper. Then unveil a large copy you have written or pass out the correct words. Each person can check his/her version with the correct one. End the session by singing "The Star-Spangled Banner."

> *It happens from September 15 to October 15.*

National Hispanic Heritage Month

Each year the United States, by Presidential proclamation, observes National Hispanic Heritage Month from September 15 to October 15. Many of our cities hold festivals at this time that feature Latin American music and dancing, foods, and arts and crafts.

Americans of Hispanic descent come mainly from Mexico, Cuba, and Puerto Rico. There are more than twenty million Hispanics in the United States today, and they comprise the second largest minority group in America. Most Hispanic Americans speak English, but many of them also speak Spanish.

The music, architecture, language, and food have had a strong influence on American culture. Hispanic-American rock group performers such as Gloria Estefan and Richie Valens have gained popularity in this country as has traditional Latin music.

Spanish architecture is popular in such states as New Mexico, Arizona, California, and Texas. Many Spanish words such as *rodeo* and *pueblo* also entered our language from these areas.

One of the strongest Hispanic influences on American culture has been food. Mexican foods such as *enchiladas, tamales, tostadas,* and *tacos* are very popular in the United States.

1. What Hispanic food do you enjoy?
2. Have you ever prepared any Hispanic foods? Do you have any recipes to share?
3. Latin music is very popular in our country. Gloria Estefan is popular and most Americans have enjoyed "The Girl from Ipanema," written by Antonio Carlos Jobim. This song has been recorded by Frank Sinatra, Tony Bennett, Sarah Vaughn, and Nat King Cole. Have you listened to this song? Do you have any favorite Latin performers/songs?
4. Have you ever danced the samba, rumba, or any other Latin dances?
5. Did you ever live in a home that had a Southwestern influence (patios, arches, viga roof beams, iron grill work)? In what parst of the country have you lived?
6. Are you Hispanic? What is your country of descent?
7. Where do most Hispanic Americans live? (The majority live in the large cities of Los Angeles, Miami, New York City, Chicago and several cities in the Southwest.)

Activity

1. Serve tacos, etc., and provide Latin music for the group to enjoy.
2. Purchase a pinata from a party store or make one. Fill it with candies, baggies full of pretzels, ballpoint pens, pencils,etc. Create gaily decorated pinatas. Use brown paper bags and decorate with construction paper cutouts, colored markers, self-adhesive stickers, and pictures from greeting cards. Divide those who wish to participate into groups of four or five. Each group can design a pinata. Hang completed pinatas as decorations.

It happened on September 16, 1620.

Mayflower Sailed for Virginia

At Plymouth, England, on September 16, 1620, the English ship the *Mayflower* sailed for Virginia. The people aboard her were Separatist-Puritans, later to be known as Pilgrims. They were the first people to come to the New World in search of religious freedom.

These Puritans had no religious freedom in England during the reign of James I, and they were persecuted for their beliefs. They had obtained an eighty thousand acre land grant from the Virginia Company. In the New World they would be able to practice their own form of worship.

The *Mayflower* carried 102 passengers plus the crew. The voyage took sixty-five days over the storm-tossed Atlantic Ocean. The ship reached Cape Cod on November 21 and dropped anchor. On that day the Puritan leaders, William Bradford and William Brewster, persuaded forty-one adult males to sign the *Mayflower Compact*. This compact formed the basis of the government that was eventually set up in Plymouth Colony. The Puritans then elected John Carver as their first governor.

One of the reasons the compact was signed was to stop the angry words of the non-Separatists aboard. These people were angry because the ship was going to land in present-day Massachusetts and not in a place granted by the charter. The compact calmed these angry people, and the *Mayflower* finally landed at Plymouth on December 26, 1620. (Later, on June 1, 1621, the Puritans received a new charter that made their settlement legal.)

The *Mayflower* stayed at Plymouth during the first terrible winter, which was filled with deprivation and disease. Over half the colonists died. On April 15, 1621, the *Mayflower* sailed for England. It arrived there on May 16.

1. The story of the *Mayflower* and those aboard her is a thrilling tale. Do you recall the first time you heard the story? Was it read to you, or did you read about in a history book? What were your thoughts concerning this daring voyage?
2. A Native American the Pilgrims called Squanto helped the settlers. Do you recall what he did? (He taught them to plant corn and to fish.)
3. What foods did the early Pilgrims have available? (Corn, venison, oysters, fish, leeks, plums, berries, goose, and turkey)
4. Eventually, in the fall of 1621, the Pilgrims gave thanks for their survival with a special meal they shared with their Native-American friends. This was the first Thanksgiving. What is something that you are thankful for?
5. Have you visited Plymouth Rock? If so, in what year? Who went with you? What did you do? What did you see when you were there?

It happens on September 17.

Citizenship Day

Citizenship Day is held each year in the United States on September 17. This is also the first day of Constitution Week.

This day honors native-born citizens who have attained voting age as well as naturalized foreign-born citizens. Citizenship Day parades and speeches point out the privileges and responsibilities of U.S. citizenship.

In 1939 many people sought a method to recognize new citizens. Newspapers across the country addressed the issue. Congress, in 1940, passed a resolution that made the third Sunday in May "I Am an American Day." People began celebrating this day.

February 29, 1952, President Harry S. Truman signed a bill that established September 17 of each year as Citizenship Day. (September 17, 1787, was the date on which the United States Constitution was signed.)

"Citizenship Day" took the place of "I Am an American Day." However, many Americans still celebrate this day in May.

A good citizen obeys the laws of his society and preserves the basic social institutions—family, religion, community, and nation. He is also considerate of the rights and needs of other citizens. He recognizes that people have different beliefs, religious or otherwise, and he respects their rights to these beliefs.

If you are a citizen, it means that this nation guarantees you certain rights and privileges and also imposes duties and regulations.

United States citizenship is obtained by birth or through a legal process called naturalization.

Are you a good citizen? Can you answer the following questions?

1. What does this nation guarantee each citizen?
2. What responsibilities do we, as citizens, have?
3. How may someone become an American citizen?
4. What was the date the United States Constitution was signed?
5. How old must a person be to vote?
6. What is the capital of the United States?
7. What is the name of the President of the United States?
8. What are the names of our two main political parties?
9. Who have been our two greatest Presidents?
10. What is the name of our national anthem?

It happened on September 18, 1830.

Horse Outran Locomotive

In a very famous race the first locomotive built in America, the *Tom Thumb*, lost to a horse on September 18, 1830. A New York manufacturer and builder of the locomotive, Peter Cooper, wanted to show officials of the Baltimore and Ohio Railroad that locomotives were faster than horses and that they should use locomotives rather than horses to pull their trains.

An engine belt slipped on the *Tom Thumb,* and it had mechanical difficulties over the nine-mile race course between Riley's Tavern and Baltimore, Maryland. A boiler leak prevented the locomotive from completing the race. However, this defeat was only a small setback for the locomotive, which in the early days of trains was sometimes call the "Iron Horse."

The first steam locomotive used for passenger and freight service in this country made its first run on Christmas Day, 1830. Steam transportation from that time on developed rapidly.

There was a very famous steam locomotive used in the Civil War. This was the *General.* Union soldiers captured it from Confederates and steamed it northward from Georgia to Tennessee. Confederate troops gave chase and finally recaptured the locomotive.

Electric locomotives began being used late in the 1800s. The Baltimore and Ohio Railroad placed the first electric locomotive into service.

The railroads in America began using diesel locomotives in the 1930s and 1940s. By 1960 the diesels had practically replaced all the steam locomotives in the United States.

Today, engineers are working to develop locomotives of greater speed and power.

1. Do you remember the first diesel locomotives? In what part of the country did you see them? What railroad were they a part of?
2. When did you take your first train ride? How old were you? Whom were you with, and what was your destination? Did you enjoy yourself?
3. Have you ridden trains much in your life? What was your most memorable trip? Why?
4. Why don't people travel by train very much today? If you had to travel across the country, what mode of transportation would you use?
5. Several towns in the United States have festivals or celebrations that present old steam-powered farm equipment or equipment used in manufacturing. Have you ever attended such festivals? What were they called, and where were they located?

Activity

Set up chairs two-by-two so part of the room resembles a train car. Participants sit in the chairs, and you walk back and forth. Pretend to be a conductor as you ask the questions.

September 19

Gettysburg Address

It happened on September 19, 1863.

Gettysburg Address

The first version of Abraham Lincoln's famous Gettysburg Address was written in Washington on September 19, 1863. Lincoln supposedly had five handwritten copies of this speech. At Gettysburg he went over the first version very carefully and then wrote a second version. It was his plan to read the second copy, and he had it in his hand while he was giving the speech. However, as he spoke, he changed parts of the speech. The biggest change was adding "under God" after the word "nation" in the last sentence. Lincoln wrote the last version of the address in 1864 and signed it. This version is carved on the plaque in the Lincoln Memorial.

The Gettysburg Address was given by Lincoln at the site of Battle of Gettysburg in Pennsylvania. The speech was delivered on November 19, 1863. The ceremonies were a dedication of a part of the battlefield as a cemetery for those men who had been killed in this battle of the Civil War. This simple speech was so powerful and eloquent that it stirs deep emotions even to this day.

At the Battle of Gettysburg, July 1-3, 1863, Confederate General Robert E. Lee faced a huge Union army under General George G. Meade. The battle began as an accident when two small opposing forces clashed. This clash turned into a terrible three-day battle. Union soldiers were positioned on the crest of a low ridge. This was the center position of the Union army. Lee had attempted to destroy the left side of the Union's defenses on the second day. On July 3, he ordered General George E. Pickett to strike at the center. Pickett's famous charge was stopped despite their reaching the crest of the ridge, and Lee began retreating to Virginia. The cause of the Confederacy was lost.

1. Discuss the life of Lincoln and his involvement in the Civil War.
2. Have you visited the site of the Battle of Gettysburg? Where is it located? Discuss what you learned there and what you remember.
3. What type of person was Robert E. Lee? Can anyone give a description of him?
4. What really caused the Civil War? Are there still ill feelings about this war in parts of our country?

Activity

Does anyone remember some or most of the Gettysburg Address? Ask someone to recite what he/she remembers of it. Then, pass out copies of the address. Let someone read the entire address aloud and then hold a discussion on its meaning and the circumstances that brought about its creation.

It happens about September 20.

Jackson County Apple Festival

From September 20-24, the Jackson County Apple Festival is held in Jackson, County, Ohio. There are mountains of apples, barrels of cider, apple butter, apple pieces, and candied apples. The attendance at this festival is about 210,000 people.

The festival is literally a riot of colors, smells, and tastes. There are countless booths filled with apple pies, apple juice, applesauce, apple jelly, and apple wine. Along with these are exhibits that display and explain a particular apple such as Golden Delicious, Delicious, Granny Smith, McIntosh, Rome Beauty, Jonathan, Winesap, Empire, Cortland, Stayman, York Imperial, Baldwin, Duchess, Early Harvest, Grimes Golden, Rhode Island, etc.

Other exhibits show and explain how apples are commercially canned, quick frozen, dried, dehydrated, made into cider, or fermented to make vinegar. Apple growers also tell you that apples consist of about 85 percent water and that they contain vitamins A and C, potassium, pectin, and fiber.

The festival-goer can buy all types of tantalizing foods made from apples as well as various kinds of apples, ciders, and wines.

1. What is your favorite kind of apple to eat—Golden Delicious, Delicious, Jonathan—or some other kind? Does one certain apple have more taste than another?
2. Which type of apple is best for making apple pie? Is it because one has a sweeter taste than another and therefore makes better pies? Which apples have a sweet taste, and which ones have more of a sour taste?
3. Did you have any apple trees growing on your property where you lived when you were growing up? What kind of apple trees were they? How were these apples used?
4. Did your mother can apples and make applesauce and apple butter? Were you a helper? What were your duties?
5. There are many recipes for apple desserts. Share some of your favorite ones.

Activity

In recent years dipping apple slices in warm chocolate sauce or caramel has become popular. At most grocery stores you can purchase tubs of chocolate and caramel that can be warmed and liquidified in a microwave. Treat the group to this new taste sensation.

It happens on September 21.

The First Day of Autumn

On our calendars the first day of autumn is September 21. However, the autumnal equinox, which marks the beginning of autumn, is really September 22 or 23. Then the rays of the sun shine directly over the Earth at the equator.

Throughout the world, autumn is celebrated as the beginning of a new year. Summer, with its vegetation (the old year) has gone, and a new year is arriving. The crops are harvested, and this indicates that a new year has begun.

Autumn is also called "fall" by many people because it is the time of falling leaves. It is also known as harvest time for many crops. In our country early autumn days are fairly warm, and the nights are cool. As winter comes nearer, the air becomes chilly, and frost occurs at night. The end of autumn exhibits the southern migration of birds, the freezing of streams, and early snow falling.

Many societies celebrate autumn as a special time. In Eastern countries, such as Japan, India, and China, rigid ceremonies and dances concerning ancestors and legends are common. Accompanying these ceremonies are large and diverse displays of food.

1. Remember autumn as a child. What were some of the things you and your family did? Were you raised on a farm? Did you take part in the harvest? What were some meals your mother prepared?
2. What is your favorite season of the year—autumn, winter, spring, or summer? Why is a certain season more meaningful for you?
3. Winter can be a very difficult time for animals. How do they survive in the cold weather? What do some of the animals such as squirrels and birds do for food and water?
4. Did you have enjoyable hobbies or activities for each season of the year? What were they? Make a list for each season.

It happened on September 22.

Ice Cream Cone Created

Italo Marchiony, who emigrated from Italy late in the 1800s, developed the ice cream cone and filed a patent for it on September 22, 1903. Italo had several pushcarts in New York City that sold lemon ice. He first developed a cone made of paper; later, he made one of pastry.

Ice cream is one of America's favorite desserts. Each person in the United States eats about fourteen quarts of ice cream a year.

Ice cream is a frozen dairy food. It contains milk products, sugar, water, and sometimes eggs. Almost all of the ice cream eaten in this country today is made by commercial manufacturers. However, many people still make their own ice cream at home.

The exact time when ice cream was first made is not known. Nero had people bring snow from the mountains for frozen desserts. The Italian Marco Polo returned from China in 1295 and brought a recipe for water ices or chilled milk desserts back with him.

This milk dessert became very popular and spread to France and England from Italy. Ice cream was brought to America by English colonists.

Ice cream became very popular in America, but most of it was made at home until 1851 when Jacob Fussell built the first ice cream plant in Baltimore. Fussell owned a milk plant. Every summer he had more milk and cream than he could put on the market, so he began making ice cream.

The 1904 World's Fair in St. Louis had ice cream cones for sale. Ice cream bars made their appearance in 1921. Today ice cream is also used in making sundaes, cake rolls, shakes, and sodas. There are dozens of ice cream flavors. Vanilla is the most popular flavor followed by chocolate and strawberry.

1. When you were a child, how much did an ice cream cone cost? How many different flavors were there?
2. Did you ever go to an old-fashioned soda fountain and have an ice cream soda? What was the name of the establishment, and where was it located?
3. Have you ever made homemade ice cream where you had to turn the crank by hand? What types did you make? What ingredients did you use?
4. What is your favorite ice cream treat? (banana split, hot fudge sundae, etc.) What kinds of toppings are available to use on ice cream?

Activity

1. Enjoy an "Ice Cream Day" where everyone samples several different flavors of ice cream. You may buy commercial ice cream or have some fun by making your own. Or, visit Dairy Queen™, Baskin-Robins™, etc., as a group to enjoy a taste treat.
2. You could also make a favorite-flavor graph listing the group's favorite ice cream.

It happened on September 23.

Birthday of Mickey Rooney

Mickey Rooney was born Joseph Yule, Jr., in Brooklyn, New York, on September 23, 1920. He first appeared on the vaudeville stage at the age of two with his parents.

Rooney's career as a child film star (1927-33) began in a series of around fifty silent comedies in which he played Mickey McGuire, a comic-strip character.

He gave heart-warming performances in the Andy Hardy series (1937-46), *Huckleberry Finn* (1939), and *National Velvet* (1944). Mickey was so popular at this time that he was named as one of the top ten money-making stars (1938-43).

His career in TV started in the 1950s, and he starred in *Pinocchio* (1957), *Leave 'Em Laughing* (1981) and *Bill* (1981) for which he won an Emmy and a Golden Globe award. He also received a Tony award for best musical actor in 1980 for *Sugar Babies*.

Rooney began performing in nightclubs in the 1960s, and in 1976 he starred in the Broadway musical *Sugar Babies*. He also continued his motion picture career by starring in such films as *The Black Stallion* (1980). In 1983 Mickey was awarded a special Academy Award, which honored his versatility as a performer.

1. Mickey was offered the role of Archie Bunker in TV's *All in the Family* before Carroll O'Connor. Do you think Mickey would have made a good Archie?
2. What are some of your favorite Rooney movies? Did you see any of the Andy Hardy movies?
3. Rooney had a long association and friendship with Judy Garland. Can you recall any of the films they starred in together?
4. Can you think of other famous child stars? (Example: Jackie Coogan)

Activity

National Velvet is available on video. Your group would enjoy seeing it.

September 24

Brittany Spaniel
Dachshund
Maltese
Akita
Bulldog
Fox terrier
Golden Retriever
Coonhound
Shih Tzu
Welsh Terrier
Chow Chow
Collie
Labrador Retriever
Greyhound
Pekingese
Scottish Terrier
Keeshond
Saint Bernard
Pointer
Afghan Hound
Yorkshire Terrier
Norwich Terrier
Lhasa Apso
Puli
Siberian Husky

> *It happens the last week of September.*

National Dog Week

National Dog Week is the last full week in September. Its purpose is to promote the relationship of dogs to mankind and to point out the need for the proper care and treatment of dogs.

The dog is truly man's best friend and was the first of man's domesticated animals. Dogs have been with man for a long time. There are pictures of dogs on the pottery of ancient Egypt, Assyria, Greece, and Rome. Many experts think the dog was domesticated somewhere in the last 15,000 years.

Dogs exist in almost every size and color. Through the years they have served man in many ways. They have delivered messages, pulled sleds, herded sheep, and rescued people trapped in the snow. Today the U.S. Army uses guard dogs, and law enforcement agencies use dogs to uncover drugs that are illegal. Dogs are also used as guides for blind people.

There have been many famous dogs. About 150 years ago there was a St. Bernard named Barry who rescued forty people trapped in the snow. He was from the Hospice of St. Bernard in St. Bernard Pass between Switzerland and Italy. Rin Tin Tin was a German shepherd who starred in nineteen movies before his death in 1932. And, there was Laika, a dog who was aboard the Russian satellite Sputnik 2 in 1957. But perhaps the most famous dogs were the collies in the Lassie movies and TV shows.

There are many interesting facts about dogs. They have forty-two-teeth—twenty in the upper part of the mouth and twenty in the lower. Smell is a dog's sharpest sense. A dog pants to cool himself. When it is hot, it pants so that perspiration from the tongue will evaporate and cool it. A dog wags its tail to let you know how it feels.

There are other interesting facts about a dog, but the main thing to remember is that if you love and care for him, he will give you loyalty and companionship in return.

1. When did you get your first dog? What was its name and what breed was it? How did you decide its name? Do you remember any special occasions with your dog?
2. As an adult, did you and your family have a dog? Where did you get it, and how did it adapt to the family?
3. How many different dogs have you had throughout your life?
4. What type of toys did your dog have to play with? Was it your job to feed and bathe the dog?
5. Was your dog an indoor or an outdoor dog?
6. Why do people have dogs? What does a dog give to a person?

Activity

1. Ask participants the names of the dogs they had. Make a list of this information and place it on a bulletin board.
2. There are many videos about dogs. The new version of *Lassie* is a classic. More modern dog films include *Beethoven*, *White Fang* and *Far from Home: The Adventures of Yellow Dog*, *The Incredible Journey*, and *Iron Will*.

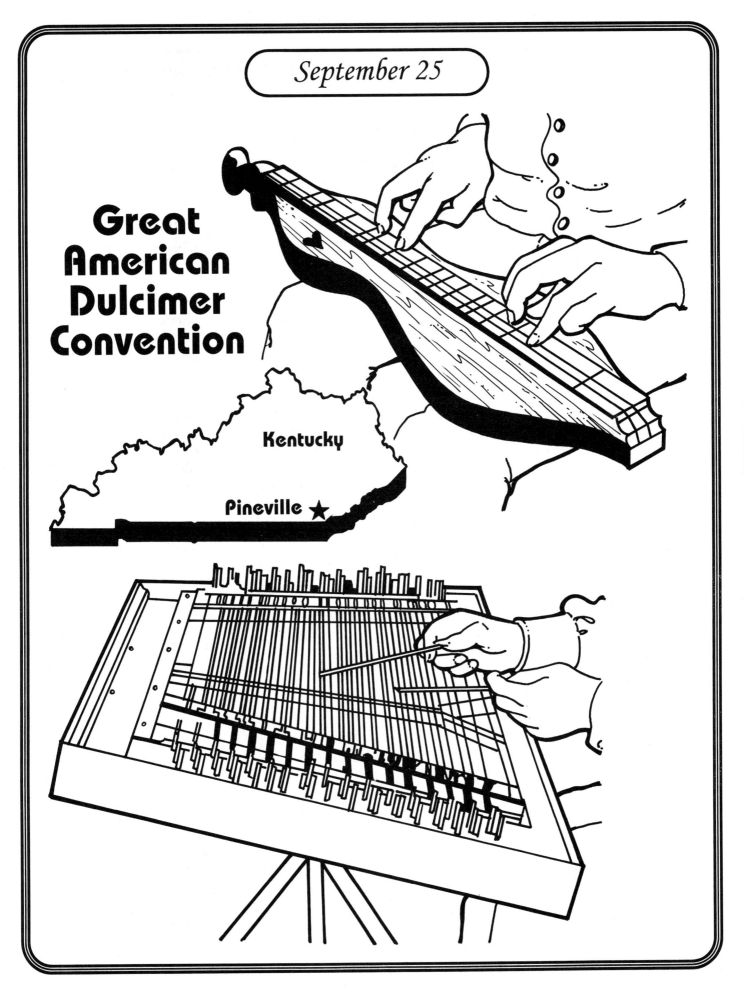

> *It happens on September 25-27.*

Great American Dulcimer Convention

The Great American Dulcimer Convention at Pine Mountain State Resort Park, Pineville, Kentucky, is held each year on September 25-27. Performers on lap and hammered dulcimers play in concert with other musicians and singers. There are also dulcimer lessons, dulcimer-building workshops, and demonstrations of crafts.

A dulcimer is a stringed musical instrument that has a light, sweet sound when played. It is used in the playing of folk songs.

There are two types of dulcimers. The plucked dulcimer, also called the Appalachian or mountain dulcimer, is shaped like a teardrop or an hourglass. This dulcimer has three or four strings and is played with the fingers. It is usually held in the lap of the player. The hammered dulcimer has two or more strings of different lengths. The strings are stretched across a flat-shaped box. The player strikes the strings with curved wooden hammers.

The hammered dulcimer was probably invented in Persia or Arabia about five thousand years ago. The plucked dulcimer was created in the United States in the 1800s from dulcimers that came from Europe. This instrument became very popular in the American folk music of the 1960s.

1. What other types of stringed instruments are found in this country? What are the types of music played on these instruments?
2. Do any of the group play stringed instruments? If so, ask them to play a song or two. Discuss the instrument and the music.
3. If anyone in your community plays a dulcimer, ask that person if he/she would be willing to perform at your facility and discuss this instrument and its uses.

(If you are interested in the Great American Dulcimer Convention and wish more information, write to Kentucky Department Parks, Capital Plaza Tower, Frankfort, KY 40601, or phone (606) 337-3066.)

Activity

If the people in your group have never played a musical instrument, you might consider allowing them to begin learning, and to, eventually, form their own band. Many retired people all over the country from fifty to seventy-six are learning an instrument and becoming band members. Rochester, New York; Madison, Wisconsin; Phoenix, Arizona; and Iowa City, Iowa have such bands. Many have been trained by graduate students from schools of music. Using volunteers from the 100-member New Horizons Band, the University of Rochester's medical school is studying whether music stimulates brain function.

It happened on September 26, 1898.

Birth of George Gershwin

George Gershwin, the renowned American composer and pianist, was born in Brooklyn, New York, on September 26, 1898. At sixteen he began writing popular songs. His first published song was "When You Want 'Em You Can't Get 'Em, When You've Got 'Em, You Don't Want 'Em" (1916), and his first song used in a Broadway musical was "Making of a Girl" from *The Passing Show* (1916).

His first hit, "Swanee" (1919), was made popular by Al Jolson. From 1920 to 1924 he wrote every song for the five editions of George White's *Scandals*. Among the songs from these and other stage works of his were "Someone to Watch Over Me," "Embraceable You," "I Got Rhythm," "I've Got a Crush on You," and "Fascinating Rhythm."

Starting with "Lady, Be Good!" (1924), the lyrics for Gershwin's songs were written by his brother Ira, and they later composed songs for cinema musicals. These included "Delicious" (1931), "Shall We Dance?" (1937), and "The Goldwyn Follies" (1938).

Gershwin was also composing serious music. His magnificent "Rhapsody in Blue" (1924) made him famous all over the world. "An American in Paris" (1928) and the opera *Porgy and Bess* (1935) furthered his famous career. Two years later (1937) he died in Hollywood.

1. "Embraceable You" is one of my favorite Gershwin tunes. Which ones do you enjoy?
2. Have you seen any musicals or films that featured songs composed by the Gershwins?
3. *Porgy and Bess* toured America and Europe after the composer's death and won acclaim. Were you fortunate enough to have attended one of these productions? If so, give us your impressions.
4. Who are some other famous American composers? Name some of their songs.

Activity

1. Play a selection of Gershwin music for the group's entertainment. Allow them to help choose the songs.
2. *Porgy and Bess* was made into a movie in 1959. It starred Sydney Poitier (Porgy), Dorothy Dandridge (Bess), and Sammy Davis Jr. (Sportin' Life). This movie is available as a video and can be shown to the participants.

> *It happens on the fourth Friday of September.*

American Indian Day

American Indian Day is the fourth Friday in September. Many thousands of years ago the people who were later called American Indians came from northeastern Asia across the Bering Strait to North America. The migration probably started at the end of the Ice Age. When Columbus reached the New World, there were thousands of Indian nations in North America. Columbus thought he had arrived in the Indies (India, China, Japan), and he called the natives "Indios," which means "Indians" in Spanish.

The Native Americans, however, did not refer to themselves as "Indians." Each tribe had its own name. The Sioux were named by the French. These Indians called themselves "Lakota-oyate." Early settlers in America named a particular tribe the Delawares. Their name for their tribe was "Leni-Lenape."

It wasn't until 1924 that most Native Americans were legally citizens. Today there are around 1,500,000 Native Americans in this country. There are 266 tribes, groups, and pueblos as well as 250 Indian languages.

In the early days of our country, there were thousands of different tribes. These tribes spoke fifty-eight major languages. Many words from these languages have become part of our American language. Common words such as *hickory*, *skunk*, *moccasin*, *squash*, *chipmunk,* and *persimmon* originated from Native-American words.

Twenty-six of our states have Native-American names. Cities such as Chicago "place of the bad smell" and Miami "people of the peninsula" have Indian names. Thousands of our rivers, streams, lakes, valleys, forests, parks, and plants also bear Native-American names.

1. Have Native Americans been treated fairly in our society? Are they accurately portrayed in movies and on TV?
2. Many tribes today earn large amounts of money through gambling casinos on their reservations. Do you think this is a good way for them to earn revenue? Have you ever been to any reservation casinos? Where were they located?
3. We have many Native-American words in our language. How many can you name? (Bayou, papoose, tepee, wigwam, wampun, tomahawk, caribou, opossum, squash, pecan, woodchuck, and terrapin.)

Activity

Can the group determine which twenty-six states have names that are derived from Native-American languages? This might be a good time to encourage research. Use encyclopedias and books about Native Americans.

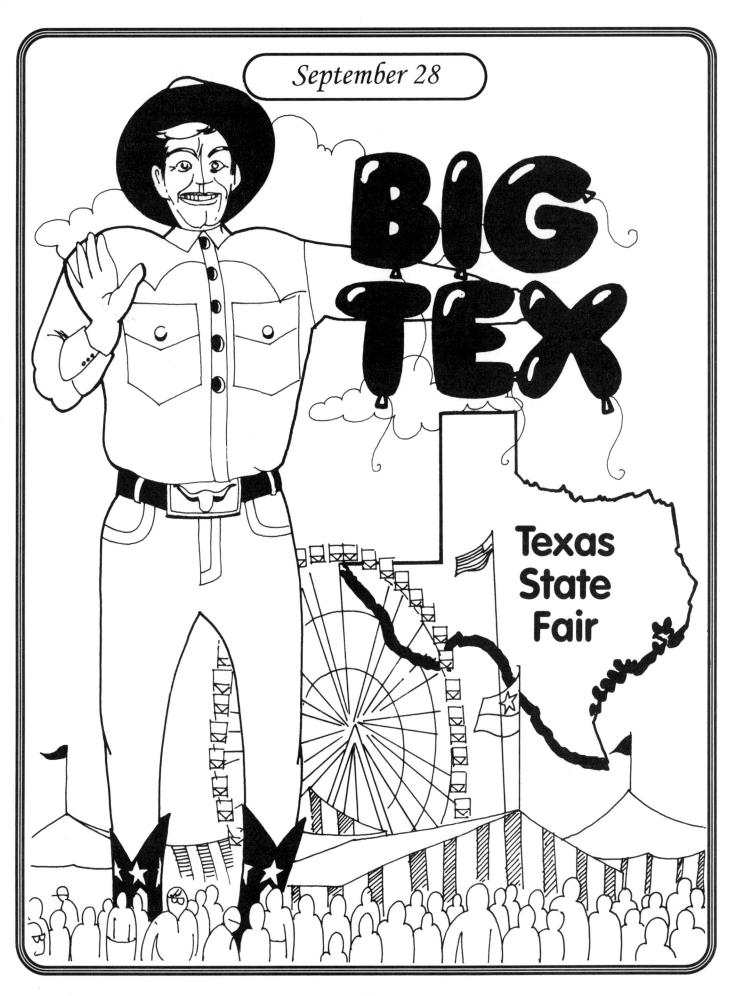

It happens between September 28 and October 22.

State Fair of Texas

The State Fair of Texas, a twenty-four day showcase of entertainment, exhibits, and competition, takes place each fall in Dallas. This fair usually runs from about September 29 to October 22 and is held in historic Fair Park. The park is a 277-acre complex recognized for its beautiful landscaping and unusual art deco architecture.

More than three million people attend this fair each year, making it one of the largest entertainment events in the world.

Cookies, cakes, jams and jellies, and other culinary delights are displayed along with examples of fine crafts and handwork. In addition, the livestock and horse shows offer various competitions each day. The fairgoers can also enjoy the best of Broadway at the Music Hall or view moon rocks from NASA, Chinese art treasures, sacred art from Ethiopia, ice spectaculars, the biggest car show in the Southwest, and daily free concerts by such artists as Randy Travis, Sawyer Brown, and the Pointer Sisters.

The main adjective associated with the fair is "big." This is immediately evident because "Big Tex," the smiling fifty-two-foot cowboy greets everyone with, "Howdy, folks!" A few hundred yards behind Tex is the Texas Star, the tallest ferris wheel in the Western Hemisphere. Next, the typical fairgoer encounters the gigantic new car show that covers two major exhibit halls. The largest stadium-laser show ever produced is a nightly feature.

Each edition of the Texas State Fair is new and different. There's a new theme every year because new shows and adventures are a main part of the fair. It is an event so crammed with variety that fairgoers can pick and choose their own entertainment and fun. Many area residents go to the fair more than one time.

1. Have you ever been to a state fair? When did you go? In what state was the fair?
2. Did you ever enter the food, craft, or livestock competition of a state fair? What did you enter? Did you win a prize or ribbon?
3. Have you ever been to Texas? Where? Have you visited Dallas, Houston, or San Antonio? Have you spent time in rural Texas? Is Texas really as big as it's said to be?
4. Some say that Texas is a place of contrasts. What do you think is meant by that statement?
5. Why do you think that Texas has earned a reputation as the biggest and the best? Do you believe this? In what ways is the statement true, and in what ways is it false?

> *It happens about September 29-October 1.*

Oktoberfest at the Amana Colonies

Every year, from the end of September to the beginning of October, a three-day Oktoberfest is held at the Amana Colonies in Iowa.

Featuring authentic German food, beer, and music, this popular fall festival presents demonstrations in woodworking, quilting, apple cider pressing, and sewing. Also included are the making of pottery, brooms, baskets, and country jewelry, microwave cooking, and craft demonstrations. Items from these demonstrations are for sale during the festival.

Along with the demonstrations, good food, and fine beer, there is continuous German music and dancing. The Edelweiss Schuhplattlers perform the Holzhacker Dance and other Bavarian folk dances. The Colony Folksingers from Amana and the Heidelberg German Band from Quincy, Illinois, continue the great German entertainment.

Other musical treats are the Alphorn duo, along with German zither players, yodelers, and piano music.

The festival runs Friday, Saturday, and Sunday, from 9:00 a.m. to 10:00 p.m. The famous Oktoberfest Parade starts at 10:00 a.m. on Sunday.

1. Have you ever attended an Oktoberfest? What was it like? Where was it? What events and exhibits did you see?
2. What types of German food have you prepared or eaten? (Sauerbraten, German meatballs, etc.)
3. Do you enjoy German music? What are some of your particular favorites?
4. There are many famous German beers. Many of these beers are known all over the world. Do you like German beer? What different kinds and brands have you tried?

Activity

Serve German strudel or Kuchen (cake) with coffee for a special social gathering for the participants. Also, provide some German music.

> *It happened on September 30.*

Babe Ruth Hit His 60th Home Run

Many baseball sports fans believe Babe Ruth (George Herman Ruth) was the greatest baseball player who ever lived. On September 30, 1927, Ruth hit his sixtieth home run.

That season of sixty home runs was something special in the baseball world. Before Ruth, no one had ever hit over twenty-four in a season. In 1927 there were 154 games in a season. Roger Maris of the Yankees set a new record of 61 home runs in a season of 162 games. That was in 1961. Ruth hit more than fifty home runs in four different seasons. He hit 714 homers by the time he retired in 1935. This record was broken when Henry Aaron of the Atlanta Braves hit his 715th home run in 1974.

Babe Ruth was born in Baltimore. His baseball career began in 1914 with the Baltimore Orioles. That same year he went to the Boston Red Sox as a pitcher. Ruth pitched 21 2/3 consecutive scoreless innings in the 1916 and 1918 World Series. During his major league career he won ninety-four games and lost forty-six.

In 1918 Ruth began to play in the outfield. He also showed he had more talent as a hitter than a pitcher. He hit eleven home runs that season. The Red Sox sold "the Babe" to the New York Yankees in 1920, and that began the golden Babe Ruth era. His personality and tremendous hitting ability attracted a huge following. Baseball became more exciting as Ruth hit home run after home run. He had so many fans that Yankee Stadium was called "The House That Ruth Built."

Ruth was released by the Yankees after the 1934 season. He played his final season with the Boston Braves in 1935. Babe Ruth was elected to the National Baseball Hall of Fame in 1936.

1. Who are some baseball players you have admired or who were considered great?
2. Did you play baseball? How long and at what position?
3. Years ago did they have night baseball games? What was the latest daylight baseball game you ever watched? What teams played in it?
4. How did Ruth get his nickname "The Babe"?

Activity

1. Show the video *A League of Their Own* starring Geena Davis. This show portrays an attempt to start a women's baseball league. Or, you could show *The Babe* starring John Goodman.
2. Match as many teams to their corresponding cities as you can:
   St. Louis–Cardinals
   New York–Yankees
   San Francisco–Giants, etc.

Daily Doses of Nostalgia
October

October			...63
October 1		Henry Ford Introduced Model-T	...66
October 2		*Peanuts* First Appears	...68
October 3		Chubby Checker's Birthday	...70
October 4		Damon Runyon's Birthday	...72
October 5		"WSM Barn Dance" Begins	...74
October 6		National Pickled Pepper Week	...76
October 7		Gold Star Chilifest	...78
October 8		The Great Chicago Fire	...80
October 9		National School Lunch Week	...82
October 10		Martina Navratilova Born	...84
October 11		National Newspaper Week	...86
October 12		Columbus Reaches the New World	...88
October 13		Cornerstone of the White House Laid	...90
October 14		Birthday of Dwight Eisenhower	...92
October 15		First Person to Ascend in a Balloon	...94
October 16		Noah Webster's Birthday	...96
October 17		San Francisco Earthquake	...98
October 18		Alaska Sold to the United States	...100
October 19		Franklin Experimented with Electricity	...102
October 20		"The Greatest Show on Earth"	...104
October 21		Great Pumpkin Festival	...106
October 22		National Save Your Back Week	...100
October 23		Gertrude Ederle Swims Channel	...110
October 24		School Teacher Goes over Falls	...112
October 25		National Magic Week	...114
October 26		Mahalia Jackson Born	...116
October 27		Birthday of Theodore Roosevelt	...118
October 28		Statue of Liberty Dedicated	...120
October 29		Birthday of Bill Mauldin	...122
October 30		"War of the Worlds" Radio Broadcast	...124
October 31		Halloween	...126

It happened on October 1, 1908.

Henry Ford Introduced the Model-T

The vehicle that changed America and the world forever appeared on the American market on October 1, 1908. It was Henry Ford's dream machine. Ford was an American original and so was his "Model-T" Ford.

Before the Model-T, all the car companies, including Ford, made only large luxury cars for the wealthy. Henry believed everyone should be able to afford an automobile, so he pioneered the assembly line and mass-produced the Model-T. Mass production meant savings in time and money, so Ford could sell his car to the American people at a price lower than anyone else. From 1908 to 1927 his company sold over fifteen million Model-Ts.

The Model-T brought in a great deal of money to the Ford Motor Company. Henry decided his workers would share in this success, so he paid each employee five dollars a day. At that time men were making a dollar to $2.50 a day. He also cut the working day from nine to eight hours.

Ford bought out the other stockholders of the Ford Motor Company in 1919 because he thought profits should be used to improve and increase the size of the company's factories. The other stockholders wanted to split the profits and make no further investment. The Ford family maintained control of the company until 1956.

In 1932 Ford develop the V-8 engine. Soon other car makers adopted this engine. During World War II he built an aircraft plant that was the largest aircraft assembly plant in the world. He also established Greenfield Village, historical buildings in Dearborn, Michigan, as well as the Henry Ford Museum. He and his son Edsel created the Ford Foundation, which has donated large sums of money to worthy causes.

1. Did anyone in your family ever own a Model-T Ford? Compare it to the cars of today.
2. Did you ever see any of the older Ford luxury cars? Can you give a description?
3. Why do you think Henry Ford cut the working day from nine to eight hours for his employees? Was it to save money or for some other reason?
4. Have you worked in a plant that produced cars? What did your job entail? Was it on an assembly line or something else?
5. See how many brand names (Ford, Hudson, Honda) of cars your group can remember. Then, see how many styles of a car can be remembered. (Ford: Fairlane, Galaxy, Thunderbird, Pinto, etc.)

It happened on October 2, 1950.

Peanuts First Appears

On October 2, 1950, Charles M. Schulz's *Peanuts* comic strip appeared in seven newspapers. *Peanuts* became the most widely syndicated comic strip. It appeared in 2400 newspapers and reached over 200 million readers a day in 68 countries. The strips were published in many languages including Italian, Serbo-Croatian, Chinese, and even Latin where Snoopy was called Snupius, and Charlie Brown was Carolius Niger.

The sweetness and humor of the strip inspired over forty television specials, four feature films, over 1400 books, and several thousand products covered with images of Snoopy, Charlie Brown, and other members of the gang. *You're a Good Man, Charlie Brown* is one of the most widely produced musicals in America. *Snoopy, the Musical* was a tremendous hit both on Broadway and in London's West End. Such *Peanuts* phrases as "you blockhead" and "good grief" have become part of our language. And "happiness is a warm puppy" is now listed in *Bartlett's Familiar Quotations*.

For over fifty years we have watched Snoopy slipping in and out of a variety of personalities, Charlie Brown trying to kick the football, Linus holding onto his security blanket, Lucy offering psychiatric advice, Schroeder being fascinated with Beethoven, and Peppermint Patty struggling through elementary school.

Despite TV specials, musicals, and books, the soul of *Peanuts* still resides in the comic strip. Charles M. Schulz, unlike several other cartoonists, drew all the figures in the over 15,000 strips published. Among the many awards of which Schulz was the recipient, three stand out: two Reuben awards from the National Cartoonists Society (Best Humor Strip and Outstanding Cartoonist) and his induction into the Cartoonist Hall of Fame.

1. Has *Peanuts* been a part of your life? When did you begin reading it? Do you have a favorite character, or do you care for all of them?
2. Charlie Brown and the gang made their television debut in the animated special, "A Charlie Brown Christmas" in 1965. Since then we have watched the "Great Pumpkin," and the "Easter Beagle," as well as shared Thanksgiving with a dinner of ice cream, popcorn, jelly beans, and pretzels, and Charlie Brown longing for the little red-haired girl. Can you remember watching any of these specials? What were they?
3. What was Snoopy before he was Charlie Brown's dog, the Flying Ace, or Joe Cool? (He was a Daisy Hill puppy where he was born into a litter of six. Marbles, Olaf, Spike, Andy, Belle, and Snoopy spent their early years as puppies at Daisy Hill.)

Activity

For the group's enjoyment, show one of the following animated specials on home video: "A Charlie Brown Christmas," "You're a Good Sport, Charlie Brown," "It's the Great Pumpkin, Charlie Brown," and "A Charlie Brown Thanksgiving."

It happened on October 3, 1941.

Chubby Checker's Birthday

Chubby Checker is an excellent example of being in the right place at the right time. He was one of several young men unknown in the music industry who had been signed to the Philadelphia Cameo-Parkway label at the beginning of the 1960s. One afternoon, quite by accident, he was in the "American Bandstand" TV studio when Hank Ballard didn't show up to sing his newest release "The Twist." Dick Clark, the show's host, searched desperately for a replacement and finally used Chubby Checker. Backed by the musicians of "Bandstand" Chubby sang "The Twist" for a vocal track in the studio and then later on "American Bandstand."

The rest is history. His version zoomed past that of Ballard's and was soon number one on the U.S. Hot Hundred. Quickly, Chubby Checker became known as the king of America's newest dance craze. By pure luck, a new star was born.

Born Ernest Evans in Philadelphia on October 3, 1941, Chubby was working as a chicken-plucker after school. One day his boss heard him sing and then asked Kal Mann, who ran Cameo-Parkway, to arrange an audition. Mann signed Evans to a contract and also gave him the stage name "Chubby Checker" after Dick Clark's wife said, "We have a Fats Domino. Let's call him a Chubby Checker."

"The Twist" entered the charts in August 1960 and eventually sold over three million copies. Its sales were fueled by Checker's tremendous personality as he danced and sang "The Twist" on "Bandstand," in newsreels, on TV, and even radio shows. He was a star. Fans followed him everywhere. For a while he was the king of rock 'n' roll.

Sales of "The Twist" faded after eighteen weeks on the charts in 1960, but amazingly came back for twenty-one weeks as number one in 1961. It is the only record besides "White Christmas" that became number one again after being off the charts for over a year.

Activity

"The Twist" is performed by twisting the hips, feet, and shoulders. It is a dance in which partners face each other but rarely touch. Many have done "The Twist" and will probably still enjoy it. Use one of Checker's recordings of "The Twist," "Let's Twist Again," "The Hucklebuck," "The Fly," or "Let's Do the Freddie" for a rock' n' roll dance party.

> *It happened on October 4, 1884.*

Damon Runyon's Birthday

Damon Runyon, journalist, author, and film writer, is best remembered for his short stories about the denizens of Broadway in the 1920s and 1930s. He developed a unique style that utilized Broadway slang and metaphors. His slick, colorful Broadway characters were the inspiration for Frank Loesser's musical *Guys and Dolls* (1952).

Runyon was born in Manhattan, Kansas, on October 4, 1884. After serving in the army during the Spanish-American War, he became a newspaper reporter in Colorado and San Francisco. In 1911 he was a sports columnist for William Randolph Hearst's the *American*. Later, during World War I, he was a war correspondent. After the war he wrote a sports column "Both Barrels" and two columns called "The Brighter Side" and "As I See It."

Starting in 1933, he began work as a screen writer. He wrote scripts for *Lady for a Day* (1933), *Little Miss Marker* (1934), and *A Slight Case of Murder* (1938). Later, he became the writer-producer in the movie *The Big Street* (1942).

Runyon's collections of stories include "Guys and Dolls" (1932), "Blue Plate Special" (1934), "Money from Home" (1935), and "Take It Easy" (1938).

1. Loesser's *Guys and Dolls* was one of the greatest hits of any musical. It ran twelve hundred performances, made over twelve million dollars, and is still being produced. It also won the New York Critics' Circle and Tony awards. Some of the show's great songs were "Guys and Dolls," "A Bushel and a Peck," "Adelaide's Lament," and "I've Never Been in Love Before." It would be a pleasant experience for the group to hear a local pianist play a selection of these songs. (*The Frank Loesser Songbook*, Simon and Schuster, New York, 1971, has these songs.)
2. Runyon was one of the greatest sports writers this country ever had. In 1932 he nicknamed Ted Radcliffe, a pitcher/catcher of the Negro League, "Double Duty." Have you ever read any of his sports articles? What can you tell us about him?

Activity

Guys and Dolls' video is available. The group might enjoy viewing it.

It happened on October 5, 1925.

"WSM Barn Dance" Begins

On October 5, 1925, WSM Radio began broadcasting in Nashville, Tennessee. One of its first programs was "WSM Barn Dance." Founded by George Dewey Hay, the program featured traditional country or hillbilly music. Two years later it was given the new name of "Grand Ole Opry" and became the longest running radio show in history.

Hay, called "the Solemn Ol' Judge," plotted the Opry's course, and the show thrived during the golden years of radio and on into the television era. Its tremendous exposure became the basis for tours of Opry stars and of Opry films.

The music of the Opry developed from different sources. In the 1920s it came from Uncle Dave Macon's ballads of rural laborers. In the '30s it continued and was influenced by the traditional music of Roy Acuff, who became a star of the Opry.

After World War II the bluegrass music of Bill Monroe and Earl Scruggs, the honky-tonk style of Ernest Tubb, the "rockabilly" music of Hank Williams, the singing of Tennessee Ernie Ford, Eddy Arnold, and Kitty Wells, as well as the comedy routines of Minnie Pearl, made the Opry even more important. Endless new stars continued the Opry's legend.

In 1941 the Opry became a live show on stage at the Ryman Auditorium in Nashville, and in 1974 the show was moved to the Opryland amusement park and entertainment center in the same town.

1. Have you ever traveled to Nashville, Tennessee, to attend the "Grand Ole Opry" show? What entertainers did you see? Can you name some of them?
2. Do you recall listening to the "Grand Ole Opry" on the radio? Can you remember what year you first heard it and how old you were at the time? What were some of the songs they were playing?
3. How has the "Grand Ole Opry" changed over the years? Who were the stars back in the '20s and '30s? Who are some of the stars of the "Grand Ole Opry" today? Make a list.
4. Minnie Pearl was probably one of the best known stars of the "Grand Ole Opry." Some people thought her brand of humor was a little "corny." What is your opinion of Minnie Pearl? Was she one of your favorite stars?

Activity

Have your own "Grand Ole Opry." Play some albums made by "Grand Ole Opry" stars such as Roy Acuff, Eddie Arnold, or Kitty Wells. Maybe some of your group would like to be a "star" themselves. You might be able to have a local Western band perform, or bring someone in to teach your group some of the new Western dances.

> *It happens around October 6.*

National Pickled Pepper Week

Pickled peppers, thanks to Mexican and Creole influence, are an integral part of the way Americans cook and eat today. They are so popular that 15,000 acres of pickling peppers are grown in the United States.

National Pickled Pepper Week, which begins on October 6, helps to celebrate this pepper's popularity and offers the following fascinating facts about pickled peppers:

> On his voyage in 1492 Columbus gave peppers their name. Searching for black pepper from the Orient, he thought the spicy pods used to flavor foods in America were a form of black pepper and by mistake called them "pimiento," or pepper. In fact, the two plants are not related at all.

> The *hot* sensation a person experiences when eating pickled peppers is caused by Capsaicin, a substance contained in the veins and inside membranes which house the seeds.

> When you eat hot peppers, the pain receptors on the tongue react and cause a physical reaction called "sweating."

Pickled peppers are a quarter of a billion dollar industry in North America.

People interviewing for a job as radio personalities are sometimes required to recite the "Peter Piper Picked a Peck of Pickled Peppers" tongue twister. To pass, they must rapidly repeat it five times without a mistake.

Some of the most popular pickled peppers are the hot jalapeno; the long, shiny, yellow banana peppers, which are sweet and hot; the red or green cherry peppers; and pepperoncini, the mildly hot green Greek or Italian peppers.

Pickled peppers make excellent garnishes, can be used in sandwiches and salsas, eaten with nachos, and can add zest to many other dishes.

1. What pickled peppers have you eaten, and with what foods were they served?
2. Do you know of any recipes that call for pickled peppers?
3. Have you ever prepared pickled peppers?
4. What is the difference between a pickled pepper and a regular pickle?

Activity

As a taste treat, serve nacho chips topped with melted cheddar and Monterey Jack cheese, a dollop of salsa, and fiery pickled jalapeno pepper rings.

While presenting and discussing this topic, you may wish to display three or four jars of pickled peppers that you have purchased at a local grocery store.

It happens around October 7.

Gold Star Chilifest

Americans love to make and eat chili. Almost everyone has his/her own recipe for it, and no one can agree on what the perfect chili consists of. No one can agree on which meat or beans are best or even if beans should be in it at all. Some prefer high-grade sirloin; others use a lean cut of beef. Some even put in a little pork or chicken. And, there is definitely no consensus on the use of red pepper sauce, cayenne pepper, or dried or fresh chiles. But, all of us agree that chili is good as long as it is hearty and tasty.

Chile, chili con carne, Texas red—whatever you wish to call this delicious mix—originated in Texas where chuck-wagon cooks made stews of chilies and seasonings for cowboys on the trail. Texas had the first cafe that sold chili before the turn of the century, and after the 1920s chili was being served everywhere west of the Mississippi.

Today there are chili contests and festivals all across America. One of the largest is the Gold Star Chilifest held at this time of the year in Cincinnati, Ohio. This festival, attended by approximately 75,000 people, includes amateur and professional chili cook-offs. Chili is the featured attraction, and all vendors are requested to serve at least one type of chili.

1. Think back to your first bowl of chili. Who prepared it—your mother, grandmother, or someone else? Did you enjoy it? What ingredients were in it?
2. Have you made chili for your own family? Did you use a special recipe? Will you share it with us?
3. Do your children use the same recipe for chili that you used? Was your recipe for chili passed down from generation to generation?

Activity

Have a chef demonstrate his/her favorite chili recipe, and then let everyone enjoy a chili supper.

October 8
The Great Chicago Fire

It happened on October 8, 1871.

The Great Chicago Fire

The Great Chicago Fire, which burned most of the city, began on the evening of October 8, 1871, on the Southwest Side.

According to legend, the fire was started by Mrs. O'Leary's cow's kicking over a kerosene lantern. Strong winds blew flames north and east throughout the city. The fire continued its destruction for twenty-four hours. It killed 300 people and left 90,000 homeless. It also caused $200 million in damages and burned a third of the city's buildings.

There have been other serious fires in this country. Two of the worst were school fires. In 1908 the Lake View Elementary School in Collingswood, Ohio, caught on fire. This terrible fire killed 178 children and adults. In 1958 another horrible fire took place at Our Lady of Angels Elementary School in Chicago. Three teachers and ninety-two children perished in that fire.

The United States has 1,200,000 firefighters. People who are paid to be firefighters must be high school graduates and must pass a civil service examination. They most also pass a physical fitness test and study first aid.

Firefighting is very dangerous. There are about 300 fires an hour in this country, and one firefighter is killed about every three days while fighting fires.

1. Do you remember reading about the Great Chicago Fire? Do you recall any certain details about this terrible fire? What do you think such a fire would cost today?
2. School fires are a serious threat. How can terrible fires such as these be prevented? What steps can be taken to eliminate these disasters?
3. The second week of October is Fire Prevention Week. Does your staff discuss fire prevention during this time? Do you have fire drills every so often?
4. Are there certain state-mandated fire safety codes? Can you name any of these? For example, how many fire exits are required for your facility? Do you know where each fire exit is located?
5. There are many courageous firefighters who are to be commended. What qualifications would you need to be a firefighter? Would you need more than just a high school education?

Activity

Invite the local fire chief to your facility to discuss Fire Prevention Week and also fire safety rules. Make a list of these rules to place on a bulletin board.

It happens around October 9-13.

National School Lunch Week

National School Lunch Week, the second week of October, celebrates good nutrition and wholesome, low-cost school lunches.

The idea of a noon meal served to children in school started in Europe. Schools in France, Germany, and other European countries began to serve school lunches in the 1800s. In 1900, Chicago, New York, and other large cities started feeding children at school, and by 1925 many schools all over the United States served lunches.

The value of a well-balanced hot lunch became readily evident to parents and teachers. As more schools participated, the federal government began assistance to school lunch operations in 1933.

In the early 1900s the National School Lunch Program provided noon meals to around twenty-four million children every day. Many children from low-income families received free meals. A similar program, the National School Breakfast Program, offered free or low-cost breakfasts during school for children in need. This program served about four million children each day.

The National School Lunch Program cost about 4.5 billion dollars a year. The National School Breakfast Program requires around 600 million dollars a year. Local, state, and federal organizations each contribute funds to support these programs.

1. A Type-A lunch supplies from one-third to one-half of a child's daily nutritional requirements and contains foods from all of the basic food groups. Can you name the basic food groups? (Breads, cereals, rice, and pasta; meat, poultry, fish, dried beans and peas, eggs, and nuts; milk, yogurt, and cheese; fruits; vegetables.)
2. Do you support these breakfast and lunch programs for schools? Why do you or why do you not think this is a good idea? There are many pros and cons for a program such as this. Can you list some reasons for and against a school lunch program?
3. Who makes up the menus for the breakfast and lunch programs? Is it the government agency on nutrition or the school cook and staff? Write down a breakfast and also a lunch menu that you think would be appropriate to serve.
4. These school lunch programs are very costly. The government is even talking about cutting down on these programs to save money. What is your view regarding doing away with the lunch program entirely?

Activity

Have your dietary department serve a breakfast and a lunch menu such as the ones served at schools. Hold a discussion to see if the group thought the meals were adequately nutritious.

It happened on October 10, 1956.

Martina Navratilova Born

International tennis became a professional sport in 1968. Because of television, professional tennis players compete for millions of dollars each year both in the United States and in many other countries. Most of the major tournaments are televised all over the world.

Leading women tennis players in the 1970s, 1980s, and 1990s have been Tracy Austin, Chris Evert, Andrea Jaeger, Martina Navratilova, and Zina Garrison of the United States; Evonne Goolagong of Australia; Gabriela Sabatini of Argentina; Steffi Graf of Germany; and Monica Seles of Yugoslavia.

Of all of these, Martina Navratilova has been the longest-lasting and the most dominant because of her powerful serve, strong backhand and forehand shots, and style of play.

She was born in Prague, Czechoslovakia, on October 10, 1956. After she defected to the United States in 1975, she applied for U.S. citizenship and became a citizen in 1981. In 1990 she won the women's singles championship at Wimbledon for the ninth time. Before her, no woman had ever won the singles' title at Wimbledon more than eight times.

Martina also won the Australian Open in 1981, 1983, and 1985. She won the French Open in 1982 and 1984 and the U.S. Championships in 1983, 1984, 1986 and 1987. In 1982 she won more than a million dollars in women's tennis. This was a new record in tennis earnings. To share her wealth with poor children, she set up the Martina Foundation. This foundation provides scholarships for the education of needy children. It also gives them tickets to tennis matches and money for tennis lessons.

Navratilova and Chris Evert Lloyd have had many exciting tennis matches against each other. In the last few years Martina has won most of the matches.

On Friday, September 25, 1992, in Las Vegas, Martina was beaten by Jimmy Connors 7-5, 6-2 in a famous tennis match before a sellout crowd of 13,832 at Caesar's Palace.

1. Martina retired in 1994, but many people still remember watching her play. Have you ever watched her, either at courtside or on television? What do you recall about her and her tennis playing?
2. Can you name some other great women tennis players?
3. There are great women athletes in many sports. Jackie Joyner-Kersee is famous in track and field. Cheryl Miller is a famous woman basketball player. Can you think of any others?
4. How much money do you think professional tennis players make? Do you think they are overpaid? Tennis is a rigorous physical sport. Perhaps they are not paid enough when you consider the pay of athletes in other sports. Discuss.

> *It happens around October 11.*

National Newspaper Week

The first or second Sunday in October begins National Newspaper Week. Reading a newspaper carefully is one of the most important lessons we can learn. Our lives are filled with news of every type every day.

Our first American newspaper was printed by John Harris in 1690. It was called *Publick Occurrences Both Foreign and Domestick*. Harris had planned to publish his newspaper once a month, but it only came out one time. He couldn't get a license because his newspaper had articles that were critical of the policies of the British.

There are approximately 500,000 newspapers in our world today. In the United States there are over 1,600 daily newspapers that have approximately 63 million readers.

Each newspaper has different elements or sections. There are news stories, editorials, feature stories, sports stories, reviews, and columns.

1. What newspaper do you enjoy the most? What section or sections are most interesting to you? Explain why.
2. Is your town newspaper a daily or a weekly? What is the name of your local newspaper?
3. Are there comic strips that you read regularly in a newspaper? Name some of your favorites?
4. Does your local newspaper have a strong sports section? Does it cover all local events and present equal coverage?
5. As a child, did you have a paper route? What paper did you deliver? Was it a morning or evening route? How did you deliver these papers? Did you walk or ride a bicycle?

Activity

Plan a trip to your local newspaper office. Ask the editor to set up a tour that will show how a newspaper is created and published. Take advantage of the opportunity to talk to staff writers, advertising personnel, and printers.

It happened on October 12, 1492.

Columbus Reaches the New World

Christopher Columbus was one of the greatest explorers of all time. He was born in Genoa, Italy, perhaps on October 31, 1451. His father was a wool weaver. He learned his father's trade, but he was always interested in the sea and went to sea when he was about twenty.

Columbus developed a theory that he could sail westward across the Atlantic and reach the Indies. In his time the Indies included Cathay (China), Cipango (Japan) and India. He asked King John of Portugal to support his project, but his request was denied. Finally, King Ferdinand and Queen Isabella of Spain said they would sponsor his trip to the Indies.

He obtained three ships fully equipped for the voyage. They were the *Nina*, the *Pinta,* and the *Santa Maria*. On August 3, 1492, his small fleet set sail for the Canary Islands.

At the Canaries the three ships headed westward across the uncharted Atlantic. On October 12, 1492, they reached the island now called San Salvador in the Bahamas. The natives, whom Columbus called Indians, traded small amounts of gold with the Spaniards. A week later the fleet reached Cuba and in December were in Haiti. There was gold there, and Columbus was excited. He thought he had reached the Indies.

Columbus made three more voyages across the Atlantic and made many more discoveries. He still thought he had found the Indies and believed so until the day he died.

1. Why is Columbus known as the discoverer of America? Why aren't the Vikings or other explorers given this credit? (It was only after his voyages that Europeans started coming to the New World to settle.)
2. When Columbus sailed to the New World, he was like an astronaut heading into the unknown in space. In what ways were his voyages different from those voyages into space?
3. How did America get its name? (The Americas or America was named after Amerigo Vespucci. Martin Walkseemuller, a German publisher, gave the new continent the name *America*.)
4. Who were some other great explorers? (Marco Polo, Vasco da Gama, Ferdinand Magellan, Captain James Cook, Dr. David Livingstone, Robert E. Peary, Sir Edmund Hillary, Jacques-Yves Cousteau, and Neil Armstrong) Can anyone discuss one of these men and his exploration?

Activity

The movie *1492* is an unusual movie that is now out in video. Show this movie and discuss it.

It happened on October 13, 1792.

Cornerstone of the White House Laid

The White House is the home of the President of the United States. It is located at 1600 Pennsylvania Avenue N.W., Washington D.C. 20025. This magnificent white stone home is a symbol of our history and unity.

The cornerstone was laid on October 13, 1792. The home was designed by James Hoban, an Irish-born architect. His design won a competition sponsored by the Commissioners of the District for the best design for the "President's House." His Georgian mansion design was modeled after the palace of the Duke of Leinster in Dublin, Ireland.

The first residents of the White House were President and Mrs. John Adams in 1800. They weren't very comfortable since work on the White House was not completed.

The White House was burned by British troops during the War of 1812. Once it was rebuilt, President and Mrs. James Monroe moved into it in 1817.

In 1902 President Theodore Roosevelt had the building repaired and built the executive wing adjacent to the west terrace.

Presidents Franklin D. Roosevelt and Harry Truman made further additions and extensive repairs to the White House. In 1961 Mrs. John F. Kennedy began to restore the White House interior to its original appearance. Mrs. Richard M. Nixon continued this effort, and later first ladies have continued this practice.

1. Have you ever toured the White House? What rooms did you visit? Were you impressed? Do you remember your thoughts?
2. Were you allowed to take pictures of the White House and its grounds?
3. Who was our President at the time of your visit?
4. What are other famous buildings located in our nation's capital? Which seems the most beautiful/interesting to you?
5. What are some other famous houses that can be visited in our various states?

It happened on October 14, 1890.

Birthday of Dwight Eisenhower

Dwight David Eisenhower enjoyed his rank of five-star general in the U.S. Army so much he even wore pajamas with five stars on the lapels.

"Ike," as he was nicknamed, was born on October 14, 1890, in Denison, Texas. In 1911 he entered the United States Military Academy and graduated in 1915. In 1916 he married Mary (Mamie) Geneva Doud in Denver, Colorado.

He was an intelligent officer and was sent to General Staff and Command School in 1925 where he graduated first in his class. Because of this, he was sent to the Army War College in Washington, D.C. By 1933 he was the assistant to Chief of Staff General Douglas MacArthur, and in 1935 he went with MacArthur to the Philippines where he was charged with improving that country's defense forces.

Eisenhower continued to advance in rank and prestige. From 1944-45 he was Supreme Commander of the Allied Expeditionary Forces. He followed this as Commander of U.S. Occupation Forces in Europe (1945). Later he became the U.S. Army Chief of Staff from 1945-48. From 1950-52 he was Supreme Commander of NATO Forces. To top all these honors, he became the 34th President of the United States (1953-1961) as a candidate of the Republican Party.

During retirement Ike, with the rank of five-star general, acted as a senior advisor to the Republican Party. He also spent time at his farm in Gettysburg, Pennsylvania or in the vicinity of Palm Springs, California. He died in 1969 and was buried in Abilene, Kansas.

1. Eisenhower really didn't care much for Douglas MacArthur's arrogant attitude and wanted him out of his command in the Philippines. Do you recall reading anything about this at the time?
2. The interstate highway system was started during the Eisenhower administration. Was this a good thing or was it bad? What changes did this bring to America?
3. The 1940s, '50s, and '60s were fast-paced times; yet, life seemed to be simpler than it is now. Do you agree with this statement?
4. Think back to 1945, the year World War II ended. What are you able to remember about that year? What did you think about the war? How many years did World War II last? Did it affect you in any way? Was it a hardship on you and your family? In what way?

It happened on October 15, 1783.

First Person to Ascend in a Balloon

On October 15, 1783, Jean Pilatre de Rozier became the first person to ascend in a balloon. In June of 1783, the Montgolfer brothers of France had sent a large paper bag 6000 feet into the air by filling it with hot smoke. Later, in September, before the assembled guests of Louis XVI and his family, these brothers sent a balloon carrying a rooster, a duck, and a sheep into the air.

Hydrogen, the lightest gas, was discovered in 1766. In August of 1783, a French physicist, J.A.C. Charles, used it to send a silk bag, thirteen feet in diameter, three thousand feet. Later that year, he and a man named Roberts went up in a balloon and stayed aloft for about two hours. This balloon was a lot like our modern round balloons. It had a valve at the top and sand ballast in the basket.

Ballooning became very popular in the late 1700s. Balloons were used in warfare by France in 1794, during the American Civil War, the Franco-Prussian War (1870-71), World Wars I and II.

The Piccard brothers of Switzerland ascended into the stratosphere in the 1930s. They went up over 50,000 feet.

A U.S. Air Force team during a series of flights in the 1950s, ascended 102,800 feet. The current altitude record was set by Commander Malcom Ross and Lieutenant Commander Victor A. Prater, Jr., of the U.S. Navy in 1961 when they ascended 113,739.9 feet.

A balloon is a bag that has been filled with a light gas or heated air. It rises because the gas or the heated air inside it is lighter and not as dense as the air surrounding it.

Balloons have many uses. Some have instruments to gather data about the weather. Others have transmitters that carry radio and television programs to remote places. Many have a basket attached underneath the balloon to carry people.

There are captive, free-floating, and powered balloons. A captive balloon is attached to the ground by a cable. A free-floating balloon goes in the direction the wind takes it. The powered balloon has an engine and propellers to create power for it. It is steered by a pilot who uses rudders and instruments to control it.

1. Free-floating balloon events take place all across the United States annually. Have you attended such an event? What was the name of it?
2. Did you ever ride in a balloon or control one? Describe the experience. Were you afraid, or did you enjoy it?
3. Pretend you are in a hot-air balloon and draw the landscape that you see below you.

Activity

To show how a balloon ascends, fill a light paper sack with hot smoke. Hot smoke goes up. The sack will too.

It happened on October 16, 1758.

Noah Webster's Birthday

Noah Webster and the word *dictionary* are synonymous. Webster compiled the first important dictionary of American English.

He was born in Hartford, Connecticut, on October 16, 1758. He served in the Revolutionary War, then graduated from Yale, was a lawyer, a newspaper editor, and a member of the Connecticut House of Representatives.

But, he was probably more interested in books than in anything else. He taught one year in Goshen, New York, and saw that American children needed better textbooks. Because of this, he wrote a book on grammar, a reader, and his famous *The American Spelling Book,* which was used for nearly a century.

In 1807 he started work on his *American Dictionary of the English Language*. He studied the connection of the English language with other languages for ten years. Then he spent seven years compiling his dictionary. This dictionary contained about 70,000 words. He finished the dictionary in 1825 and published it in two volumes in 1828.

In his dictionary Webster chose the best American usage of the time. He differed slightly from English forms of the words and chose the simpler of two spellings when he felt like doing so. He wrote *develop* instead of *develope*, *theater* instead of *theatre*, etc. It is because of Webster that we spell many of our words differently than the British.

1. In what ways—both as a child and as an adult—have you used a dictionary?
2. What can be found in a dictionary other than definitions of words? (Abbreviations, biological names, geographical names, punctuation, usage, college addresses, etc.)

Activity

1. Supply the group with dictionaries. Working in pairs, have them define and look up the origins of these words: lunar, jovial, tantalize, and nocturnal.
2. Ask them to think of words that begin with the Greek stem "mono" (one). (Monologue, monopoly, monomania, etc.) Do the same with "bi" (two). (Bicycle, biped, bilateral, etc.) You can also do "poly" (many), "theo" (god) and "anthropo" (man).

(Does your facility have a large-print dictionary? It would be an excellent addition to the library.)

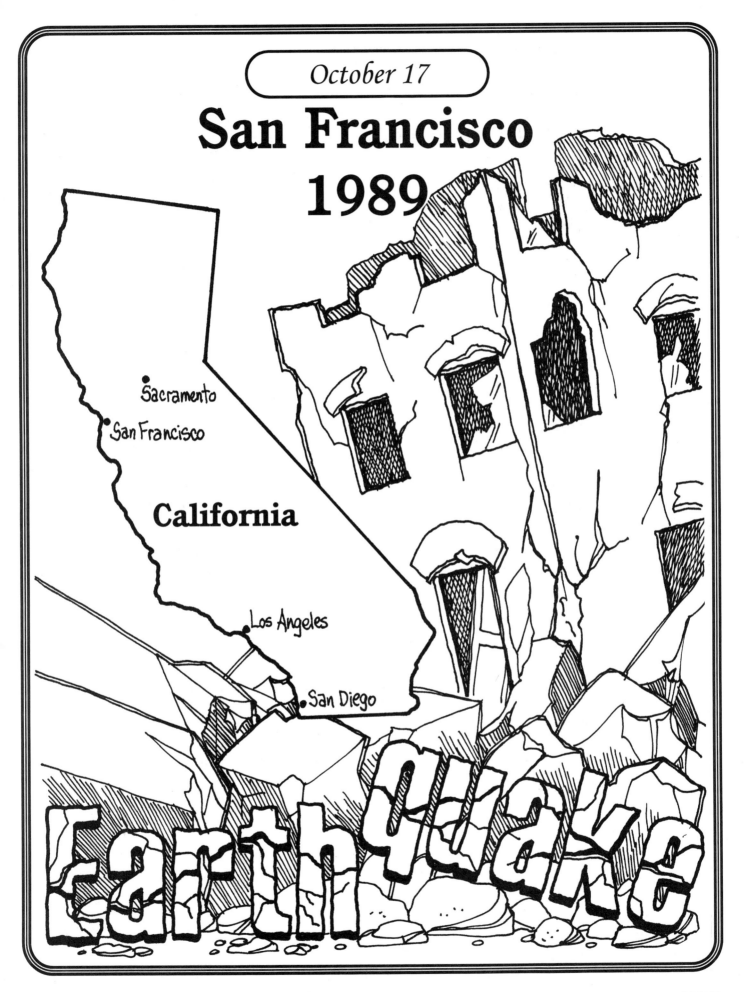

It happened on October 17, 1989.

San Francisco Earthquake

On October 17, 1989, a strong earthquake shook the city of San Francisco and its immediate area. It caused the deaths of thirteen people and three billion dollars in property damage in San Francisco County.

The worst earthquake San Francisco suffered occurred in April of 1906. The earthquake caused gas mains to explode, electric wires to break, and gas lamps and stoves to overturn. Because of these, fire broke out and roared through the city for three days. The city lay in ruins. Property damage was over $500 million, over 250,000 homes were destroyed, and 3,000 people lost their lives.

Besides these earthquakes in California, there have been earthquakes all over the world. An earthquake is a violent shaking or shock in the earth. A large earthquake's energy release may be 10,000 times as powerful as an atomic bomb.

Earthquakes occur when the earth's surface, composed of seven large plates and many smaller ones, shifts and ruptures. These plates are in continuous motion. The motion stretches and squeezes rocks at the edges of the plates. When the force gets too great, it causes an earthquake.

The energy an earthquake releases travels away from the fault in seismic waves (vibrations). Near the center of the earthquake, these seismic waves can be extremely destructive. As the waves move away from the center, the vibrations become weaker. Seismologists (people who measure and record the vibrations within the earth) study these seismic waves to pinpoint the location of an earthquake.

Exact predictions of earthquakes are not possible, but scientists know in which regions earthquakes will occur by studying the history of earthquakes all over the world. They are able to estimate how many years apart earthquakes will occur in one area.

1. Were you ever in an area when an earthquake occurred or had occurred? Discuss what you remember.
2. California may expect a terrible earthquake once every fifty to one hundred years. Would you remain in California if you lived there? Why or why not?
3. Kobe, Japan, had a huge earthquake on Tuesday, January 17, 1995. There were a reported 3,109 dead, 645 missing, and 15,277 injured. Japan is one of the most seismically active areas of the world. This accounts for Japan's experiencing around 1,000 earthquakes a year—most of them minor. What help do people need after such an earthquake? (Medical aid, food, water, fuel, and shelter)
4. What are other types of similar disasters?

It happened on October 18, 1867.

Alaska Sold to the United States

Alaska didn't always belong to the United States. It was a Russian possession. The Russians established claim to it in 1741 and set up their first trading posts there in 1784.

Russia attempted to sell this territory to the United States in 1855. It was finally sold to us on October 18, 1867, during the presidency of Andrew Johnson. The man responsible for the United States' buying this vast territory was Secretary of State William H. Seward. The price paid for this territory was $7,200,000. Senator Charles Sumner, a colleague, supported the measure and said our new possession should be named Alaska, "great land." (This is from an Aleut word that also means "mainland.")

Many Americans thought Seward had made a mistake in buying Alaska. They thought we had paid too much for a land that was probably not worth much. They called Alaska "Seward's folly" or "Seward's icebox."

Time has proven these people wrong and Seward right. The vast land of Alaska is filled with endless resources of oil, natural gas, gold, iron ore, coal, platinum, vast forests, and rich fishing grounds.

For forty years Alaskans wanted to become a state. They worked for more than forty years for statehood. On January 3, 1959, President Dwight David Eisenhower signed the statehood proclamation, and Alaska officially became the 49th state.

Alaska is our largest state. It is twice the size of Texas. Its total area is around 586,412 square miles, and its coastline is 6,640 miles in length. Alaska also has four major natural regions: (1) the Arctic Slope, (2) the Rocky Mountain System, (3) the Interior Plateau, basin of the great Yukon River, and (4) the Pacific Mountain System.

1. Alaska is a beautiful state. Have you traveled to any part of Alaska? Where did you go? Did you travel as a family?
2. Have you been on the great Alaskan Highway? Were you pleased with its construction and the tourist facilities along the way?
3. Do you think you would like living in Alaska? (Some parts of it only have a few hours of daylight each day.)

Activity

Show a travel video of Alaska.

> *It happened on October 19, 1752.*

Franklin Experimented with Electricity

Benjamin Franklin was one of the greatest men this country has produced. He was an author, a printer, a public leader, a statesman, a scientist, and an inventor. He was the only man who signed four of the most important documents in our history: the Declaration of Independence, the Treaty of Alliance with France, the Treaty of Paris with Great Britain, and the Constitution of the United States. Of Franklin, it can truly be said that he did many things and that he did them well.

As a scientist, he was a leader in the world in experimenting with electricity. In Philadelphia on October 19, 1752, he carried out his famous experiment with electricity. Flying a homemade kite in a thunderstorm, he proved beyond a doubt that lightning is electricity. Lightning struck the kite wire and ran down to the key tied at the end. There it caused a spark.

Franklin invented the lightning rod to control lightning. This was a device used to protect houses and other buildings from being damaged by lightning. The lightning rod was a metal rod placed on top of a building. A cable or wire led from the rod to a ground wire that was buried ten or more feet in the earth. His lightning rod is still used today.

Besides his experiments with electricity and his invention of the lightning rod, Franklin invented a stove that was more efficient in heating. His invention of bifocal eyeglasses was beneficial to many people. He also showed that acid soil could be improved by using lime. He was the first scientist to chart the course and record the temperature, depth, and speed of the Gulf Stream in the Atlantic Ocean.

Franklin published his *Poor Richard's Almanac* from 1773 to 1778. The fame of the almanac rests chiefly on the wise and witty sayings that Franklin scattered through each issue. Discuss the meaning of the following statements:

1. "God helps them that help themselves."
2. "He that falls in love with himself will have no rivals."
3. "Little strokes fell great oaks."
4. "Early to bed and early to rise, make a man healthy, wealthy, and wise."
5. "Keep thy shop, and thy shop will keep thee."

Activity

Can you think of other witty sayings such as "A little learning is a dangerous thing" and "Fools rush in where angels fear to tread"? Make a list of these sayings that the group remembers, and place them on a bulletin board.

It happened on October 20, 1873.

"The Greatest Show on Earth"

The circus goes back thousands of years. The Romans held circuses that featured battles between warriors; they also had chariot races. The Circus Maximus in Rome seated over 180,000 people.

During the 1700s the modern circus developed in England and soon spread to America. These early circuses were small and featured clowns, jugglers, and riding acts.

The 1800s was the golden age of the American circus. Around ten large circuses toured the country. One of these circuses, established in 1871, belonged to the fabulous showman Phineas T. Barnum. His was the most famous circus of the time. On October 20, 1873, his circus, now called "The Greatest Show on Earth," opened in his Hippodrome in New York City.

From 1844 to 1847, before he opened his circus, Barnum made a fortune by touring with a midget named General Tom Thumb. In 1850 and 1851, Jenny Lind, a famous singer from Sweden, was managed by Barnum. And, in 1882, Barnum brought over a huge elephant called Jumbo from the London Zoo. This elephant performed in his circus.

Barnum did everything to build his circus into the biggest and finest. He hired top acts and advertised widely. He was also involved in many publicity stunts that drew interest to his circus.

His circus moved across the country in railroad cars. This was a new idea. Before that, a circus moved from town to town in wagons drawn by horses.

Barnum later had a partner by the name of James A. Bailey, and the circus, larger than ever, was called the Barnum and Bailey Circus. Barnum died in 1891, and after Bailey died in 1907, the circus was bought by the Ringling brothers. The Ringling Brothers Circus and the Barnum and Bailey Circus were merged in 1919. Today, even though the Ringling family sold the circus in 1967, it is still known as the Ringling Brothers and Barnum and Bailey Circus.

1. Did you ever attend a circus performance? What do you remember? What animals did you see? What tricks did they perform? What animals caught your attention the most? Why?
2. What age were you when you first attended a circus? Did you go with your parents? Who accompanied you? How did you get there? How long did you stay?
3. Did you ever get anything at a circus that became a favorite item—something such as a stuffed animal?
4. How many circuses have you been to? What is the largest circus you ever saw? Have you taken your own children or grandchildren to a circus? How did they respond?

> *It happens around October 21-22.*

Great Pumpkin Festival

The pumpkin originated in Mexico around 7000 to 5500 B.C. This vegetable, which is related to squash, has plants which produce round or oval fruits whose shells are hard and hold coarse, stringy pulp. The main cavity in the fruit contains the seeds. The average pumpkin weighs about thirty pounds, but some can weigh over eight hundred pounds. Most pumpkins are orange, but some varieties are yellow, white, or other colors.

Pumpkins contain a rich supply of potassium and vitamin A. Some farmers use pumpkins to feed their livestock. In the United States people enjoy the pumpkin cooked in pumpkin pie, or they enjoy making jack-o'-lanterns for Halloween.

Pumpkins grow on vines and bushes that have huge leaves. They grow best in slightly acid soil and usually take four months to ripen. These plants need to be carefully cultivated to produce healthy fruit. Pesticides and mosquito netting is used to prevent insect plant damage.

To celebrate and honor the pumpkin, Bedford, Pennsylvania, holds its Great Pumpkin Festival on October 21-22. There are record-breaking pumpkins to be seen, and growers can bring their own pumpkins for weigh-ins and cash prizes. There are also carving or painting a jack-o'-lantern contests, live entertainment, a costume parade, and making a scarecrow and pumpkin-pie eating contests.

1. Pumpkins come in all different sizes. There are no two pumpkins alike. What is the largest pumpkin you have ever seen? Describe it. How much do you think it weighed?
2. Name some other vegetables, besides pumpkins, that have a rich supply of vitamins. What are the vegetables, and what vitamins do they contain?
3. What certain holiday is associated with pumpkins? Can you tell us why? What do people do with pumpkins on this holiday? Describe one or more of the pumpkins that you had for this certain holiday. What did you do with it?
4. A lot of people grow their own pumpkins. Did you have a garden or pasture where you grew your own pumpkins? Explain how to grow them, and tell us what your pumpkin patch looked like. Were they all one color?
5. Do you know who came up with the idea of making jack-o'-lanterns out of pumpkins? Did you ever enter a jack-o'-lantern contest or a pumpkin-pie eating contest at a Pumpkin Festival? Did you win a prize? Describe these events.

October 22

Save Your Back Week

It happens during the fourth week of October.

National Save Your Back Week

Congress is being asked by many concerned citizens and physicians to declare the fourth week in October as National Save Your Back Week.

According to several specialists in physical medicine and rehabilitation, back pain places a great strain on the nation's health and economy. Eighty percent of our population will experience back pain. Back pain costs an estimated fourteen to thirty billion dollars each year. This represents health care costs and lost wages.

While there are many possible causes for back pain, physicians believe improper care of the back is an important one, and they offer the following tips to place less strain on the back, and, by so doing, reduce back pain:

1. When possible, bend at your knees and not at your waist if you are picking something up.
2. Don't bend at the waist without using a hand to help you move something or reach something.
3. Be as close to an object as possible when lifting it. Do not lift something far away from your body.
4. Lift an object slowly and steadily. Do not jerk.
5. Keep your body straight. Have good posture. Don't slouch.
6. If possible, don't lift a heavy load.
7. When you get out of bed, roll over on your side and push up with your hands. Do not get up by sitting up straight.
8. If you do sit-ups, keep your knees high—not straight.

Physicians also make the point that these principles are to help prevent back pain—not treat it. If you have back pain, you should consult a doctor.

Activity

List these tips on back pain prevention on white poster board and tack it on the bulletin board. Then, every so often, go over these tips and discuss them with the group. If possible, ask a physician, nurse, or physical therapist to discuss back pain prevention.

October 23

Gertrude Ederle Swims the English Channel

It happened on October 23, 1906.

Gertrude Ederle Swims Channel

The English Channel, the body of water between England and France, connects the Atlantic Ocean and the North Sea. It is 350 miles long and twenty-one to one hundred miles in width. It is also the busiest sea passage in the world.

For hundreds of years, the English Channel has been important. Julius Caesar sailed up the Channel looking for oyster beds and tin mines. The Anglo-Saxons sailed across it in their invasion of England. And, William the Conqueror led his Norman invaders over it in his conquest of England.

People have always been aware of the Channel. Many ships have sailed on it. Swimmers have sought to conquer it. One swimmer, an American named Gertrude Ederle, who was born on October 23, 1906, in New York City, swam it when she was nineteen. She was the first woman to do so. In 1926 Gertrude swam from Cape Grisney, France, to Dover, England. Her time of thirty-five miles in fourteen hours and thirty-one minutes broke the previous world record.

Before she set the Channel record, Ederle had already set twenty-nine U.S. and world records from the 50-yard to the half mile. She was also a gold medal winner at the 1924 summer Olympics Games where she was a member of the championship U.S. 400-meter free-style relay team.

In 1978 Penny Lee Dean of the United States set a record in swimming from England to France. Her time was seven hours and forty minutes. Other swimmers still attempt the Channel, but the most important event concerning this body of water began in 1986 when Great Britain and France made plans to begin construction of a railway tunnel under the Straight of Dover. The digging began in December 1987 and was completed in May 1994. Now called the Eurotunnel or the Channel Tunnel or Chunnel, this 31-mile-long, 150-feet-deep tunnel (actually three parallel tunnels: two for trains plus a service tunnel) links Folkestone, England, with Calais, France.

1. Did you watch Penny Lee Dean on TV as she swam the Channel in 1978?
2. Share with us any memories you have in regard to swimming. How old were you when you first swam? Who taught you to swim? Did you swim in a pond, lake, beach, or elsewhere?
3. Which do you think is better for exercising: swimming or walking? Why? What other type of exercises can you do to benefit your health?
4. Have you crossed the English Channel by ship? What year was this? Where did you sail from, and where did you arrive?

It happened on Octber 24, 1901.

Schoolteacher Goes over Falls

Niagra Falls, whose name comes from the Neutre Indians and means "thundering water," are two waterfalls on the border between the United States and Canada. They are the forty-ninth highest in the world and the third greatest in the volume and power of water that pours over them.

The falls are located about the middle of the Niagra River which divides the United States and Canada. On the American side the 1,050 feet wide river flows over the American Falls and drops 184 feet. On the Canadian side the river flows over the 2,215 foot wide Horseshoe Falls and plunges 176 feet.

The magnificent beauty of the waterfalls makes them one of the top tourist attractions of North America. Many couples have gone there on their honeymoon, and others have attempted to become celebrities by going over the Falls in a barrel.

The first to survive a trip over the Falls was a widowed schoolteacher named Anna Edison Taylor. On October 24, 1901, she went over the Falls in an oak barrel that had cushions in it. She suffered gashes and a concussion, and when she crawled out of the barrel, she stated that "Nobody ought ever to do that again."

Taylor, who was forty-three years old and couldn't swim, thought she would make a great deal of money giving speeches about her exploit, but she was a terrible speaker and never made any money.

Many people have died attempting this feat, and it is now against the law.

1. What is it about Niagra Falls that attracts a lot of honeymooners? What does love have to do with it? Can you think of a reason? Did you go to Niagra Falls on your honeymoon?
2. There are other beautiful waterfalls in the United States besides Niagra Falls. Can you name any of them? Have you ever seen any of them? If so, where and when?
3. Do you think when you were growing up that you would ever have been brave enough to try going over Niagra Falls in a barrel? Share with us your thoughts about this.
4. Are waterfalls an act of nature, or are they man-made? What makes the running water so powerful?
5. What makes many waterfalls such top tourist attractions? Is it because the beauty of the waterfalls is breathtaking? What about the sound of the rushing water? Does it remind you of something else?

It happens during the last week of October.

National Magic Week

National Magic Week is celebrated the last full week of October. The Society of American Magicians adopted the idea as a way of promoting the Art of Magic and, at the same time, performing shows at hospitals, orphanages, and nursing homes for those who would have difficulty getting to see a live performance.

It all started as "Houdini Day" in the summer of 1927. There were many other "Houdini Days" that followed, but it was not until 1938 that, with Mrs. Houdini's permission, October 31 was proclaimed as National Magic Day in honor of Harry Houdini. It was not not long after this when National Magic Day became National Magic Week.

Now, each year, governors, mayors, and other governing bodies throughout the country are requested to issue proclamations declaring the last week of October as National Magic Week. Magicians throughout the country are encouraged to partcipate in the activities. Many people enjoy magic shows during this week.

Magic displays can be found at libraries, stores, and malls throughout the country during National Magic Week.

When the week is over, each local assembly of the Society of American Magicians compiles its week's activities and submits them to the National Council of the Society of American Magicians where they are judged. Awards are presented at the National Convention held each year in July.

1. Have you ever seen Harry Houdini performing his magic in a movie short? When was this, and what did he do?
2. Why do you think Houdini is considered to be the greatest magician who ever lived?
3. Who are some magicians you have watched perform?
4. Have you ever done any magic tricks? What were they? Can you still do them?

Activity

1. Ask a local magician to perform and discuss his tricks.
2. Watch a David Copperfield TV special on magic.

> *It happened on October 26, 1911.*

Mahalia Jackson Born

Mahalia Jackson became the most famous gospel singer in the world. Her powerful singing expressed dignity and strong religious feelings. She didn't like being associated with nonreligious music although her singing style had a great deal in common with that of the great blues and jazz singers. One of her greatest performances was with The Duke Ellington Orchestra in 1958 when she sang "The Twenty-Third Psalm" as well as Ellington's "Come Sunday."

Born in New Orleans on October 26, 1911, Mahalia sang in the church choir for her father, who was a minister. She moved to Chicago in 1928 where she worked in a food plant and as a hotel maid. She also became the soloist in a Baptist church. By 1930 she was recording and touring across the United States.

In the 1940s Jackson was becoming very popular, and in the 1950s she became world famous during several international tours. In the 1960s she was sick at various times and had to be hospitalized in 1967 and later in 1971. She died on January 27, 1972, in Evergreen Park, Illinois.

A music critic, Dan Morgenstern, sums up Mahalia: "Her art, projected with immense dignity and vital power through the magnificent instrument of her voice, is one of the glories of black-American music in this century, and it reached and touched untold millions.

Some of her best-known LPs are "What the World Needs Now," "I Believe," "Garden of Prayer," "Bless This House," "Power and Glory," and "Mighty Fortress."

In 1975 an excellent biography, *Just Mahalia, Baby,* by Lurraine Goreau was published by World Books of Waco, Texas.

1. Was Mahalia Jackson's singing style mostly gospel, or was she also associated with other forms of music? What were they?
2. Mahalia Jackson performed with The Duke Ellington Orchestra in 1958. Did she also perform with any other orchestras? If so, can you name any of these orchestras?
3. Who are some other black gospel singers? Are there any white gospel singers who are as good as Mahalia Jackson? Who are they? Do you enjoy gospel music?
4. Did you ever collect any of Mahalia Jackson's gospel albums? What were some of the songs? Do you remember any of the words to any of her songs? Sing or hum a couple of lines.

Activity

Have a gospel sing-a-long session. Play some of Mahalia Jackson's albums and let the group sing along as they listen to the music. Or, you might have a pianist come in to play gospel music for the group's entertainment.

It happened on October 27, 1858.

Birthday of Theodore Roosevelt

Theodore Roosevelt was the youngest President in the history of the United States. When President William McKinley was assassinated in 1901, Vice President Roosevelt took office. He was forty-two.

Roosevelt proved to be an extremely colorful person. He was affectionately called "Teddy" or "T.R." by most Americans. The voters elected him to a second term as President in 1904. In 1912 he ran for President a third time as the "Bull Moose" party candidate, but lost.

He was born in New York City on October 27, 1858, to a wealthy family. He was puny as a boy and suffered from asthma. His father built a gymnasium in their home, and the boy exercised regularly. His body became strong, and he had tremendous physical strength.

After he was graduated from Harvard in 1880, Theodore attended law school at Columbia University for a short time, but he wasn't interested in the courses.

He decided to enter politics and served three terms in the New York state assembly. Then, to get over the deaths of his wife and mother in 1884, Roosevelt left politics. He purchased two cattle ranches on the Little Missouri River in the Dakota Territory. The hard ranch life helped him to forget his sorrow.

He returned to New York in 1886 to run for mayor, but he was defeated. Then, he worked several years for the U.S. government. Later, he worked for two years cleaning up crime in New York. After that, he was Assistant Secretary of the Navy for a short time.

In 1898 he resigned his naval position when the United States declared war on Spain. He became the commander of the First Volunteer Cavalry Regiment that rode into battle in Cuba. These men, former cowboys and athletes, became known as the "Rough Riders." They and Roosevelt became national heroes.

In 1898 Roosevelt was elected Governor of New York. Later he became the vice president of the United States. Then, when McKinley was killed, he became President.

As President, he built America into a world power and brought strict government control over industry and large business monopolies. He won the Nobel Peace Prize in 1906 for helping to end the Russo-Japanese War.

1. What is your image of Theodore Roosevelt? (President, hunter, Rough Rider, Nobel Prize winner.)
2. The Teddy Bear was named after Theodore Roosevelt, whose nickname was "Teddy." In 1902 Clifford Berryman drew a cartoon for the *Washington Evening Star* of Roosevelt refusing to shoot a baby bear. Soon this bear became "Teddy's bear." Then, a Russian immigrant to America, Morris Michtom, created a toy bear and put the name "Teddy's bear" on it. Soon he was selling all he could make. Also in 1902, in Germany, a lady named Margarete Steiff made a bear that was sold in America. This bear was also called "Teddy." (Did you have a favorite teddy bear when you were small? Was he a gift? How old were you?)

Copyright © 1996 Gary Grimm & Associates

It happened on October 28, 1886.

Statue of Liberty Dedicated

The statue *Liberty Enlightening the World* stands on Liberty Island in New York Harbor. This fantastic copper sculpture of a robed woman holding a torch, one of the largest statues ever built, is a symbol of freedom to all of the world.

The people of France presented the Statue of Liberty to the American people in 1884. This gift was a symbol of the friendship between the two countries and of the ideal of liberty both people shared. The people of France donated around one million francs to build the statue, and Americans raised $250,000 to construct the pedestal. Frederic Auguste Bartholdi, a young Alsatian sculptor, designed the statue and picked out its site. The statue was dedicated on October 28, 1886.

From its feet to the top of the torch, the statue stands approximately over 151 feet. It weighs 225 short tons. The figure is composed of more than three hundred copper sheets, 3/32 of an inch thick. It is supported by an iron framework designed by Alexandre Gustave Eiffel, the French engineer who built the Eiffel Tower in Paris.

On the pedestal is a famous poem by Emma Lazarus entitled "The New Colossus." This was inscribed in 1903 and reads as follows:

> Not like the brazen giant of Greek fame,
> With conquering limbs astride from land to land;
> Her at our sea-washed, sunset gates shall stand
> A mighty woman with a torch, whose flame
> Is the imprisoned lightning, and her name
> Mother of Exiles. From her beacon-hand
> Glows world-wide welcome; her mild eyes command
> The air-bridged harbor that twin cities frame.
> "Keep ancient lands, your storied pomp!" cries she
> With silent lips. "Give me your tired, your poor,
> Your huddled masses yearning to breathe free,
> The wretched refuse of your teeming shore.
> Send these, the homeless, tempest-tost to me,
> I lift my lamp beside the golden door!"

1. What does the Statue of Liberty symbolize to the people of America and to the rest of the world?
2. There has been a great outcry recently about America's accepting any more new immigrants. An example of this is our refusal to allow any Haitians to enter this country and, to some extent, any Cubans. What has brought about this new attitude? Do you think it destroys the very concept the Statue of Liberty stands for?
3. Were you born in America, or did you come to this country as a child with your parents? If you did emigrate, what was your country of birth? What year did you arrive here, and what were your first impressions of the United States?

It happened on October 29, 1921.

Birthday of Bill Mauldin

Willie and Joe were two of the most memorable cartoon characters of World War II. These two war-weary G.I.s viewed heroism and the military with quiet cynicism and were very popular with the everyday serviceman. However, many officers, particularly General George Patton, viewed Willie and Joe as a slap in the military's face.

These two cartoon characters, who portrayed the American G.I.s view of combat life during World War II, were drawn by Bill Mauldin, who was an artist for the *45th Division News* and the army newspaper *Stars and Stripes*. He covered the fighting in Sicily (where he was wounded), Italy, France, and Germany.

Mauldin, who was born on October 29, 1921, prepared for his artist career by attending the Chicago Academy of Fine Arts in 1939. In 1940 he joined the Arizona National Guard and trained for the infantry. He was sent to Europe in 1943.

Willie and Joe made Mauldin famous, and he won a Pulitzer Prize in 1945 and a second one in 1958. His cartoons were published in the *Star-Spangled Banner* (1941 and 1944), *Mud, Mules, and Mountains* (1944), and *Up Front* (1945).

After Mauldin got out of the service in 1945, he became a syndicated cartoonist. He was an actor in the films *Teresa* in 1950 and in *The Red Badge of Courage* in 1951. Later he was an editorial cartoonist for the *Saint Louis Post-Dispatch* and then for the *Chicago Sun-Times*.

1. Cartoons are an enjoyable entertainment for people of all ages. Are they an enjoyment for you? Which cartoon characters make you laugh? Do any of them make you also feel sad? Why?
2. Can you recall seeing and reading the Willie and Joe cartoon that was created during World War II? What was this cartoon trying to portray to the servicemen? Did you agree with this portrayal, or do you think the creation of this cartoon was done in poor taste?
3. What about the artistry of this cartoon? In your opinion, was this cartoon well-drawn? Can you define the different types of art? What does it take to be a good artist?
4. Is there a difference between being a syndicated cartoonist and an editorial cartoonist? Can you explain what difference, if any, there would be?
5. It takes only one cartoon to make an artist famous. Can you name any other cartoon artists? Make a list of the names of the cartoons and also the names of the cartoons' artists.

> It happened on October 30, 1938.

"War of the Worlds" Radio Broadcast

On October 30, 1938, Orson Welles made his famous "War of the Worlds" radio broadcast. In the broadcast, Wells, an actor and later a motion-picture director, discussed a fictional invasion of New Jersey by Martians. People in the eastern United States were terrified. They thought Earth was being invaded by Mars. Thousands of people called the police and government officials.

This broadcast continued our interest in and love of science fiction. Movies, novels, and comic books portrayed aliens from outer space coming to Earth or attacking Earth, and the interest has never stopped.

One of the most interesting subjects of science fiction is the flying saucer or UFO (unidentified flying object). Thousands of UFOs have been sighted by people since the end of World War II. Many people believe these UFOs are spaceships from other planets. They have been described as being saucer-shaped and moving at high speeds. Many times they have been described as flying just above the ground and rising quickly.

The U.S. Air Force and scientists working for them have studied photos of UFOs and say they have logical explanations. They are weather balloons, meteors, satellites, etc. But, many people won't accept this. Even pilots, both commercial and those flying in combat, have spotted these strange, lighted flying saucers. People who won't accept the Air Force's explanation have formed their own groups to study UFOs.

In the spring of 1977 our interest in science fiction was really given a boost when a film called *Star Wars* was released. This film, the first in a movie trilogy named the *Star Wars Saga*, was the epic story of a young man named Luke Skywalker whose purpose was to save the galaxy from conquest. Along with Princess Leia, Hans Solo, and others, Luke continued the fight in the next two movies, *The Empire Strikes Back* and *Return of the Jedi*. This was the most popular series in movie history and ranks among the top films ever made.

1. Did you hear Orson Welles' famous broadcast in 1938? What was your reaction to it? How did other people respond?
2. Many people have been quoted as saying that they have sighted UFOs. Have you seen one? Did others doubt you? Did you report the sighting to the media or the government? Did you belong to a UFO group?
3. Is our government hiding the fact that there really are flying saucers? If they are, what is the reasoning behind it?
4. The voyages of "Apollo" from 1969 to 1972 represent the greatest exploration of all time. There were seven "Apollo" voyages and billions of dollars were spent on this project. Was the United States justified in spending such amounts of the taxpayers' money? What do you think these space flights accomplished? Should there be more flights to Mars and beyond?
5. *Star Trek* is extremely popular. Many of us identify with Captain Kirk, Mr. Spock, Dr. McCoy and other members of the *U.S.S. Enterprise*. Have you been a *Star Trek* fan? Do you still watch it with its newest members? Are you a "Trekkie"?

It happens on October 31.

Halloween

Halloween, that fun-filled event, takes place on October 31. It is a time of ghosts, goblins and witches, of pumpkins, trick-or-treating, and Halloween parties. It is also a time when many children trick-or-treat for UNICEF (United Nations International Children's Emergency Fund), a custom that began in 1950. The money collected for UNICEF helps buy food and medicine for poor children in Third World countries.

Halloween means "hallowed or holy evening" because it's the day before All Saints' Day. A long time ago, people began celebrating All Hallow Even (evening) on October 31. As time passed, the name became Halloween.

There are many superstitions and symbols connected with Halloween. The ancient Druid priests of Britain and Gaul thought that witches, ghosts, spirits, and fairies came out on Halloween to cause harm to people. From these beliefs comes our use today of witches, ghosts, and goblins in Halloween celebrations.

There is an Irish tale about the origin of the word "jack-o'-lantern." A man named Jack couldn't go to heaven because he was miserly and mean. He also could not go into hell because of practical jokes he had played on the devil. So, according to the tale, he is still walking the earth with his lantern until the end of time.

Colonists from England brought their Halloween customs to America. They gathered together on this night to tell ghost stories, bob for apples, and have fun singing. Halloween was a time for playing pranks that were harmless.

1. Did you ever pull a mischievous Halloween prank on someone? Were you happy you did it, or were you ashamed afterward? Do you want to reveal this mischievous prank?
2. What is your favorite recollection of Halloween? Will you tell us about it? What are some of the details of this event?
3. What were some of the Halloween costumes you had over the years? Did your mother make and design them, order them out of a catalog, or purchase them in some other way? Discuss the design of some of your costumes.

Activity

1. With group involvement, plan a Halloween party. Each person makes his/her own costume and mask. (A mask can be made using a paper plate or a paper bag that is decorated with yarn, paint, and colored paper.)
2. Have a jack-o'-lantern design contest. Each person draws a jack-o'-lantern. Select three or four of the best designs. Anyone who wishes can choose one of the designs to carve into a pumpkin. After the pumpkins have been carved, place lighted candles in them, and then display them in different locations of the facility.

Daily Doses of Nostalgia
November

November 127

November 1	Election Day	130
November 2	North Dakota and South Dakota Admitted into the Union	132
November 3	John Montague Born	134
November 4	Birthday of Will Rogers	136
November 5	Roy Rogers Born	138
November 6	Birthday of John Philip Sousa	140
November 7	National Split Pea Soup Week	142
November 8	Margaret Mitchell Born	144
November 9	Berlin Wall Opened	146
November 10-12	Waterfowl Festival	148
November 11	Veterans Day	150
November 12	First Professional Football Player	152
November 13	Birthday of Robert Louis Stevenson	154
November 14	Favorite Author Day	156
November 15	Georgia O'Keeffe Born	158
November 15-21	National Geography Awareness Week	160
November 15-21	American Education Week	162
November 18	Christmas Festivals	164
November 19	Birthday of Tommy Dorsey	166
November 20	National "Red Kettle" Kick Off Day	168
November 21	Invention of the Phonograph	170
November 22	Assassination of John F. Kennedy	172
November 23	Birthday of Billy the Kid	174
November 24	Oscar Robertson Born	176
Fourth Thursday of November	Thanksgiving Day	178
November 26	Sojourner Truth Born	180
November 27	Twenty-Seven More Shopping Days	182
November 28	First Woman Elected to Parliament	184
November 29	Birthday of Louisa May Alcott	186
November 30	Mark Twain Born	188

It happens on the first Tuesday of November.

Election Day

Election Day occurs on the first Tuesday after the first Monday in November. This is the day on which national elections for President and Vice President take place. The day was selected by Congress in 1845 and has been the same day since then.

On this day other kinds of elections are also held. There are elections for governors, state legislators, county officials, local officials, and members of boards of education.

Before the general election there are primary elections to choose Republican, Democratic, and other party candidates to run for office in the general election. There can also be a run-off election if no candidate wins a majority in the general election. Then, there are special elections to vote in new people for officials who leave office before their term is up or for those who die while serving.

On election day a registered voter goes to a designated building in a precinct in which he/she lives. There the voter receives a ballot from an election clerk. Then, the voter goes into a voting booth and marks his/her ballot. The ballot is given to the clerk, and the ballot is folded and placed in a ballot box. If a voting machine is used, paper ballots are not used.

The only people who could vote in this country before 1868 were white males. Our Fourteenth Amendment allowed black males their voting rights. Females in the United States could not vote until the Nineteenth Amendment was passed in 1920.

Voting is a sacred right and obligation in the United States. We are a united people, and each of us has the right, through voting, to make our desires heard and acted upon.

1. Can you recall the first time you voted in a presidential election? Who were the candidates? How old were you when you first voted?
2. Perhaps a member of your family might have run for a government office. If this is true, share your remembrances of this special and exciting time in your life. Did you help with the campaign? In what capacity?
3. Why do you think campaigns cost so much money? There are many fundraisers for each candidate and party plus private donations, etc. What do you think should or could be done to eliminate a lot of the cost of running for a government office? Give us some of your ideas or thoughts about this.
4. What is your opinion about people voting either a straight Democratic or Republican ticket? Do you think this is right, or should you vote for the candidates of your choice regardless of their party?
5. How has election day changed from when you first voted? Give us some details.

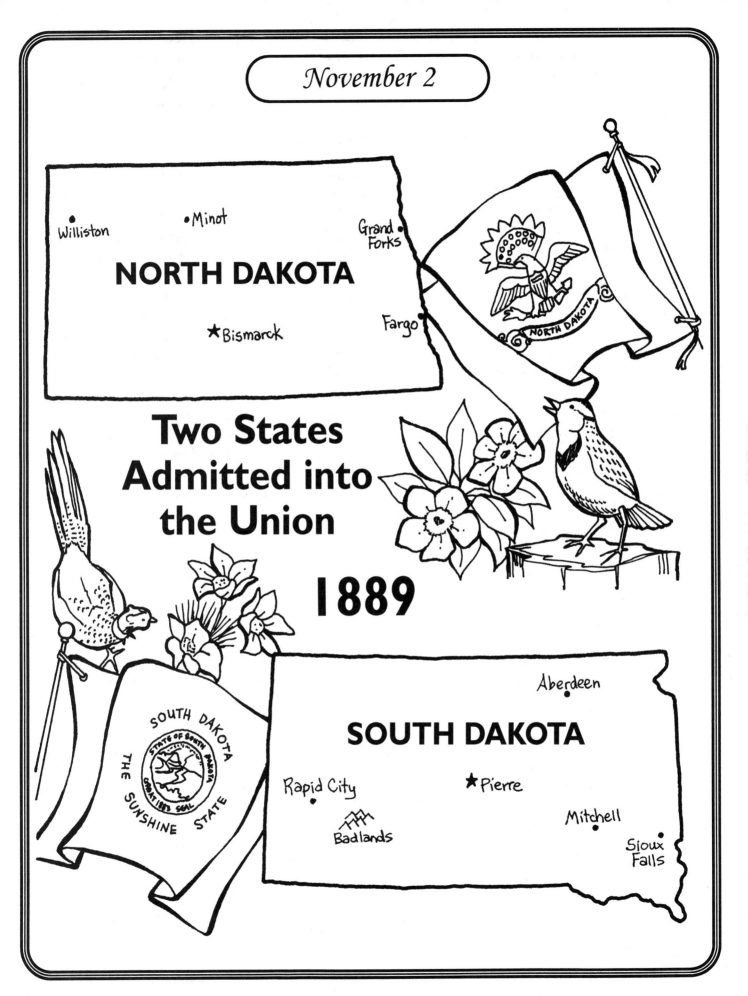

It happened on November 2, 1889.

North Dakota and South Dakota Admitted into the Union

The midwestern states of North Dakota and South Dakota, are locked together in history. On November 2, 1889, when both states were ready to be admitted into the Union, President Benjamin Harrison shuffled the admission papers so that one state could not claim it entered the Union before the other one. Today, the two states are ranked alphabetically. North Dakota is the thirty-ninth state and South Dakota is the fortieth.

Both states were named for the Sioux Indians, who once lived in the region. The Sioux called themselves *Dakotas* or *Lakota*, meaning "friends" or "allies." One of North Dakota's nicknames is the "Sioux State." It is also called the "Peace Garden State" after the International Peace Garden that lies partially in its borders or the "Flickertail State" because of the flickertail squirrels that live there. South Dakota, because of its sunny climate, has the nickname of the "Sunshine State." It is also known as the "Coyote State."

Many tourists visit the two states each year. One popular place is the Theodore Roosevelt National Park in the beautiful Badlands. It is a wildlife sanctuary in North Dakota. Two other visitors' favorites in North Dakota are the International Peace Garden that lies partly in North Dakota and partly in Manitoba, Canda; and lake Sakakawea, the reservoir for the Garrison Dam, one of the world's largest earth-fill dams.

Many Americans have visited South Dakota's two favorite tourists' destinations. One of these is the Mount Rushmore National Memorial. There, the sixty-feet-high-heads of George Washington, Thomas Jefferson, Theodore Roosevelt, and Abraham Lincoln have been carved out of the granite mountain. The other favorite visitors' site is Crazy Horse Memorial near Custer, South Dakota. This is a gigantic sculpture of the renowned Sioux chief. Korczak Ziolkowski carved this figure out of the granite mountain. He began in 1948 and worked until his death in 1982. Members of his family continued his work.

1. Do you have any connections to either the state of North Dakota or the state of South Dakota? Do you recall ever having visited either state? Do you have a relative living in one of the states?
2. If you had to drive to North Dakota from where you lived, how many miles would you have had to drive? What states would you drive through? How long would it take you to drive there? How about South Dakota? (Answer the same questions for that state.) Compare the distances for the two states.
3. Can you locate North Dakota and South Dakota on a map? Are the two states right next to each other? Which is the more populated state?
4. If you were going on a vacation and you had the choice of choosing between the two states, which state would you prefer visiting? Give us your reasons for your choice?

Activity

Make a list of the various visitors' sites in both states. Under each site, write a few sentences telling us what you think you might see at each site. Which ones do you think would be the most fascinating?

It happened on November 3, 1718.

John Montague Born

The word *sandwich* is very interesting. We all know what a sandwich is. It is a slice of bread that is covered with meat, cheese, or other mixtures which is finally covered with another slice of bread. In fact, the sandwich was invented by John Montague, the Fourth Earl of Sandwich, who was born on November 3, 1718. He was England's first Lord of the Admiralty. While playing cards in a twenty-four-hour-long gambling session in 1762, he invented the sandwich when he ordered a servant to bring him two slices of bread with a piece of roast meat between them.

Sandwich is also connected to or with other words. There is a sandwich board, a sandwich coin, and a sandwich man. There were also at one time the Sandwich Islands. When Captain James Cook landed at modern Waimea on Kauai in January 1778, he named the archipelago the Sandwich Islands in honor of John Montague, England's Lord of the Admiralty. We know these islands as the Hawaiian Islands.

Besides these sandwiches, there is a Sandwich, Massachusetts; a Sandwich, Illinois; and Sandwich, a borough in England in Kent on the Stour River. Do you know of any others?

1. There are lot of different ways to make a sandwich. What is your favorite sandwich? Is it some type of lunchmeat, or is it a mixture of ingredients? Describe your favorite sandwich.
2. Sandwich shops are still in existence today. There are many names associated with sandwich shops. Two examples would be "cafe" or "coffee shop." Can you name any others? Are you familiar with subway sandwiches?
3. Identify the various types of sandwiches that would be served in a sandwich shop or cafe. What kind would you usually order?
4. When you made sandwiches at home, did you use white bread, whole wheat bread, or some other kind? Do you know what fingertip sandwiches are? How do you make them?
5. If you were ordering a hamburger, what condiments would you use—pickles, catsup, mustard, onion, relish?

There are other interesting facts concerning the names of food. The hamburger was originally Hamburg steak named after Hamburg, Germany. The frankfurter is named after Frankfurt, Germany. These sausages were first made in the Middle Ages. An American vendor selling cooked frankfurters in 1900 called them "hot dachshund sausages." Later the term became "hot dogs." Pizza is an Italian name for pie, and this food originated in Italy.

It happened on November 4, 1879.

Birthday of Will Rogers

Will Rogers was an American humorist and homespun philosopher. He was also one of the greatest ropers of all time. Will started life as a cowboy and then became a star on stage and in the motion pictures. But, he is remembered today for his homely witticisms such as, "All I know is just what I read in the papers."

He was born on a ranch in Indian Territory (later the state of Oklahoma) on November 4, 1879. His parents had some Cherokee Indian blood, and he was always proud of it. Many times he stated, "My ancestors may not have come over on the *Mayflower*, but they met 'em at the boat."

Will learned to perform rope tricks when he was young. He began working as a cowboy in the Texas panhandle and later went to Argentina and South Africa in search of adventure. In South Africa he became a star in a show titled "Texas Jack's Wild West Circus."

In vaudeville he was a trick roper and a humorist. During his rope-twirling, he told jokes and made comments about our society. People laughed at his jokes and enjoyed the wisdom in them.

Will became very popular and made his first appearance on stage in New York City in 1905. In the Ziegfeld Follies of 1916 he became very famous, and he made his first motion picture in 1918. In 1920 he was writing a column that appeared in newspapers across America. In addition, he wrote many magazine articles and authored six books. With his Southwestern drawl and shrewed wit, he became a personality on the radio, in the movies, and as a lecturer.

He was killed in a plane crash near Point Barrow, Alaska, while on a flight to the Orient with the aviator Wiley Post. At the time of his death, he was loved and honored all over the world.

Will Rogers was known for his tremendous sense of humor. He attempted to take something true, exaggerate it, and make it funny. Discuss the meanings of his following statements: (Grammatical errors are his!)

   a. "Every time Congress makes a joke it's a law. And, every time they make a law, it's a joke."
   b. "We are all igerant, only on different Subjects."
   c. "We hold the distinction of being the only nation that is goin' to the poorhouse in an automobile."
   d. "There's one thing no nation can accuse us of—that is secret diplomacy. Our foreign dealings are an open book—a checkbook."
   e. "I am just an old country boy in a big town trying to get along."

1. What qualities did Will Rogers possess that made him so popular with all types of people?
2. What was it in his background that made him strive so?

> *It happened on November 5, 1912.*

Roy Rogers Born

Roy Rogers, the "King of the Cowboys," was born on November 5, 1912, to a poor family. He never completed high school and worked in a shoe factory in Ohio and as a fruit picker in California. His family loved music, and Roy, when he was young, learned to play the guitar and mandolin and to sing and yodel.

Republic Pictures was auditioning for a singing cowboy, and Rogers won the role and became the most famous singing cowboy actor of all time. He was the number one box office Western star for twelve consecutive years and starred in eighty-seven Westerns for Republic. In his films he rode his faithful golden palomino Trigger. In thirty of his films his co-star was the former band singer Dale Evans, who became his wife in 1947. He, Trigger, and Dale always stopped the bad guys, and his films were pure and wholesome. Every film included his singing talents.

Rogers has been very productive all of his life. He organized the Western group "Sons of the Pioneers" in 1932 and starred in his first movie *Under Western Stars* in 1938. His TV show "The Roy Rogers Show," ran from 1951-57 and made him a fortune in the licensing business. Children from all over the United States dressed as Roy Rogers' Little Buckaroos with gun belts, cowboy hats, T-shirts, and pajamas. He has also hosted the TV show called "The Great Movie Cowboys" (1975), made numerous appearances at rodeos and fairs, been a recording artist for Capitol Records, and been involved in many large business ventures.

Fans still flock to see Roy and Dale when they make public appearances at rodeos, parades, fairs, and theaters. Roy was voted into New York's Madison Square Garden's Hall of Fame. He set an all-time, one-day box office record there.

Today he spends most of his time at the Roy Rogers–Dale Evans Museum in Victorville, California, where he often greets fans in his white hat and cowboy clothes.

1. Why was Roy Rogers called "King of the Cowboys"? What did he do to deserve this reputation?
2. Do you know if there was a reason for Roy's horse being called Trigger? Give a description of Trigger. What was Trigger's role in all of Roy's movies?
3. Roy starred in at least eighty-seven Western movies. Can you identify some of these movies?
4. Dale Evans was Roy's leading lady in more than half of his movies. In what type of role was she usually cast? Compare Dale Evans to some of his other leading ladies. What made her also become a star?
5. Since Roy Rogers and Dale Evans made a lot of public appearances in rodeos, fairs, parades, etc., did you ever see them in person? What were your impressions of them? Share with us your remembrances. Was Roy wearing his white cowboy hat and cowboy clothes? What was Dale wearing?

It happened on November 6, 1854.

Birthday of John Philip Sousa

In 1900 the American writer Rupert Hughes stated, "There is probably no other composer in the world with a popularity equal to that of John Philip Sousa." Sousa was a famous composer and band leader in the United States. He wrote different kinds of music including songs, waltzes, operettas, orchestral suites, and his famous marches, which made him known all over the world as the "March King."

Sousa, who was born on November 6, 1854, in Washington, D.C., began his career at the age of seventeen, playing in dance and theater orchestras and going on tour with a variety show. He played in Jacques Offenbach's orchestra in 1876 when the French composer made a tour of America. After that, Sousa wrote the first of his many operettas.

In 1880 he was made the leader of the U.S. Marine Corps Band. Many of his famous marches were written for this band, which soon became known as one of the finest bands in the world. Sousa got his discharge from the Marine Corps in 1892 and soon formed his own band.

This band became very famous, and Sousa was honored around the world. In 1910 and 1911 he and his band made a world tour that was extremely successful. In 1917 he began a two-year career as the band leader for the U.S. Navy.

Sousa's military marches were very rhythmic and filled with vitality. He composed 136 marches. Some of these were "The Stars and Stripes Forever," "The Washington Post," "Semper Fidelis," and "The High School Cadets." Besides music, he wrote an autobiography and five novels.

1. I'm sure you have head of the U.S. Marine Corps Band. Is this a jazz band, a marching band, or other? Can you name some of the marches they played? Make a list.
2. If you attended a dance where the U.S. Marine Corps band would be performing, what dances or dance steps would you be doing? Maybe you could even show us some dance steps that you remember.
3. Waltzes used to be a favorite dance several years ago. Did you ever attend a ballroom dance? What other dances would you be doing besides the waltz? Describe the ballroom gown that you might be wearing. They still show ballroom dancing contests on television. Do you enjoy watching them?

Activity

Play some of John Philip Sousa's famous marches such as "The Stars and Stripes Forever" and "The High School Cadets." Have the participants march in step to the music either by standing in place or parading around the room or even down the halls. This would also be a great exercise program.

November 7

Split Pea Soup Week

It happens around November 7.

National Split Pea Soup Week

The lowly pea, beloved by farmers and home gardeners alike, is one of America's best and most versatile foods. Rich in protein and vitamins A and C, it is used in soups, casseroles, salads, or eaten separately.

This important seed legume is native to the Old World and was one of the first domesticated plants. Its use as a food can be traced back as far as 7000 B.C.

The pea, grown mostly in cool regions (especially in China, northern Europe, parts of Russia, and the northwestern United States), is a plant grown mainly for its round, edible seeds, which are also called peas. There are two main types—field peas and garden peas. Field peas have smooth, hard seeds that may be yellow, green, white, gray, brown, blue, or spotted. Some varieties of yellow and green field peas are marked as *split peas* (peas which have been dried and had the outer skin removed) for making soup.

Prepared correctly—flavored with herbs and enriched by the addition of pork—split pea soup is a culinary delight. This dish is so popular that there is a National Split Pea Soup Week held every year around November 7-13.

1. If you had a garden, did you grow garden peas? Can you describe what they looked like?

2. How were these garden peas used in your food dishes? Can you recollect any of your recipes that called for garden peas? Did you ever prepare fresh peas and young potatoes?

3. If you were to eat the peas just by themselves, how would you prepare them? How would you flavor them?

4. Were peas one of your favorite vegetables? Did you ever eat split pea soup? Did you like it? Can you give us a description of what the taste was like?

Activity

Provide copies of *Ladies' Home Journal*, *Good Housekeeping*, and *Family Circle* for your group to look through to see if they can find different recipes that include using peas.

> *It happened on November 8, 1900.*

Margaret Mitchell Born

Most Americans recognize the name Margaret Mitchell. This famed author of *Gone with the Wind* was born in Atlanta, Georgia, on November 8, 1900. Her mother was the president of the Atlanta Historical Society, and Margaret was raised in a home concerned with local history. She attended Smith College for one year, but after her mother's death she returned home to Atlanta to care for her father and brother.

She was married in 1925, and for the next ten years she wrote about the stories of the Civil War and the Reconstruction she had listened to as a child. These developed into a historical novel of over a thousand pages. This book, published in 1936 as *Gone with the Wind*, was the only novel she ever wrote.

Gone with the Wind, winner of the Pulitzer Prize and the National Book Award, was a publishing marvel. It set a sales record of fifty thousand copies sold in one day and 1.5 million copies sold the first year it was published. It was translated into over thirty languages. Victor Fleming's film, based on the book, starred Clark Gable and Vivien Leigh. It was released in 1939 and is possibly the most popular movie ever made.

Margaret Mitchell died in 1949 after being struck by an automobile in Atlanta. Her *Gone with the Wind Letters: 1936-1949* was published in 1976. Alexandra Ripley continued the story of Mitchell's book in *Scarlett: The Sequel to Margaret Mitchell's Gone with the Wind*. This was published in 1991.

1. Have you read *Gone with the Wind*? Did you enjoy it? Can you tell us what the novel is about? Who is your favorite character?
2. Did you go to see *Gone with the Wind* when it first came out as a motion picture? What do you remember about it? Do you recall the theme song "Tara"?
3. Have you ever written anything that was published? Tell us about it and how long it took for you to write it.
4. At any time have you ever wanted to be a writer? What would you like to write about? Have you thought of a good name for a novel?
5. Did you ever win any writing awards in high school or college? What were the awards for?
6. What really caused the Civil War? How was this war different from a war between two different countries?

It happened on November 9, 1989.

Berlin Wall Opened

The Berlin Wall was built in 1961 to divide the city of Berlin into two parts. These were Communist East Berlin and non-Communist West Berlin. East Germany, backed by Soviet Premier Nikita S. Khrushchev, built the Berlin Wall to stop East Germans from emigrating to the West.

The Berlin Wall was about twenty-six miles long and was constructed of concrete slabs that ran from twelve to fifteen feet in height. Barbed wires and pipes were placed on top of most of the Wall. There were also mines, trenches, barbed wire, armed guards, and police dogs to discourage escape attempts. Other barriers were also built around the rest of West Berlin. All the barriers totaled about 110 miles.

Before 1961 many East Berliners had walked from East Berlin to West Berlin seeking freedom and higher standards of living. The Wall stopped them. Around ninety people were killed attempting to escape from East Berlin by going over or crossing the Wall.

In 1989 there were widespread uprisings in East Berlin from people who demanded more freedom. Many East Germans fled to the West by way of Austria and Hungary. On November 9, 1989, the East German government opened the Wall and ended all travel and emigration restrictions. The East Germans started tearing down the Wall. All of the Wall and the other barriers would eventually be removed. In 1990 East and West Germany became a single country once again, and Berlin was once more a single city.

1. Did any of you ever have the chance to travel to Berlin, either when it was one city or after it was divided? What were your impressions of this city?
2. Were any of you occupants of Berlin when the Berlin Wall was built in 1961? How did you feel about the city being divided? What kind of problems did this wall create?
3. Can you give a description of what this wall looked like? Was it guarded at all times? Why did they need to do this?
4. The Berlin Wall divided numerous families. How many years do you suppose it was before many families were reunited? How would you feel if this had happened to your family? Describe what your feelings might be?
5. The Berlin Wall was finally torn down in 1989. Imagine yourself standing at the Wall as it was being opened for travel once again. What would be going through your mind knowing that the elimination of this wall would mean freedom for millions of people. Just think what a joyous occasion it would be to see your loved ones again. Can you describe the joy of this imaginary moment in detail?
6. How is a backyard fence similar/different from the Berlin Wall?
7. Have you ever been denied the freedom to enter or leave a country?

November 10

Annual Waterfowl Festival

It happens on November 10-12.

Waterfowl Festival

The annual Waterfowl Festival, November 10-12, is a great weekend event in the historic hunting area of Easton, Maryland. This premiere wildlife art show is a showcase for nationally recognized artists, decoy carvers, photographers, and artisans. There are over five hundred exhibits of antique duck decoys, waterfowl paintings, photographs of wildlife scenes, waterfowl carvers, shooting displays, retriever demonstrations, and workshops. Attendance for the festival is over twenty thousand.

In the Blue Room and the Gold Room, there are magnificent paintings by the premiere wildlife painters in the United States. Their paintings have been selected by a jury as the best of hundreds sent in. The paintings are bid on, and the artists' works are sold. A small fee is paid to the Waterfowl Festival by each artist on any artwork sold.

The Waterfowl Festival is unusual for its mission of supporting waterfowl and wildlife conservation through research, education, and habitat preservation. Since its inception in 1971, this volunteer, nonprofit organization has provided education and entertainment for thousands of people and has donated around three million dollars to waterfowl education and conservation.

1. Do you think our wildlife and wetlands are threatened? What can you do as an individual to help save them?
2. Why do you think it is necessary that we preserve our wetlands and waterfowl for future generations?
3. Do you enjoy the outdoors? Have you spent a great deal of time camping, hunting, or fishing? What is it about a wilderness setting that enlivens a person?
4. Do you enjoy wildlife and waterfowl? If you were an artist, what would be your favorite waterfowl to paint? Imagine yourself sitting by a pond on a nice, warm spring day watching the waterfowl and enjoying the scenery. Do the sights and sounds give you a peaceful feeling? Describe your emotions.

> It happens on November 11.

Veterans Day

Veterans Day honors all of the men and women who have served in the armed services of the United States. President Woodrow Wilson, in 1919, proclaimed November 11 as Armistice Day to commemorate an end to the fighting in World War I. But, it wasn't until 1938 that this day became a national holiday. Congress changed the name to Veterans Day in 1954, and President Dwight David Eisenhower signed the bill into law. It was to be a day to honor veterans and a day dedicated to world peace.

On this federal holiday celebrations include parades, speeches, prayer services, and flag displays. Special services are conducted at the Tomb of the Unknown Soldier in Arlington National Cemetery, Arlington, Virginia.

There are three main veterans' organizations in the United States. These are the American Legion, the Veterans of Foreign Wars, and the Disabled American Veterans. These organizations assist needy veterans and their widows and children, see that veterans' rights are upheld, that hospitalization and medical care are provided for their members, organize memorial services for veterans who are deceased, support patriotism and community activities, develop comradeship among their members, and honor the men and women who served their country.

1. This day is a very emotional time for all veterans. Why is this? Did any of your family serve in the armed services? How did you feel when a member of your family was drafted? How did it affect your family life?
2. There are many parades and ceremonies on Veterans Day each year. Do you remember attending any of these parades or ceremonies? Were there marching bands and speeches? Recount some of your memories of any of the Veterans Day parades?
3. Have you or any member of your family belonged to any of the veteran organizations? If so, which one? In what ways did this veterans' organization assist needy veterans and their families? Can you remember a particular instance in which you helped a veteran? What did you do?
4. Where is the Tomb of the Unknown Soldier located? In what state? Do you recall the name of the cemetery?

Activity

Invite a veteran of Desert Storm, the Vietnam War, or the Korean War to visit your facility. Allow plenty of time to ask questions.

It happened on November 12, 1892.

First Professional Football Player

William "Pudge" Heffelfinger became the first professional football player when he was paid twenty-five dollars for expenses and a bonus of five hundred dollars on November 12, 1892. The cash bonus made him a professional. He scored the game-winning touchdown as his team the Allegheny Athletic Association beat the Pittsburgh Athletic Club by the score of 4-0.

The first professional game—where all the players were paid—was in 1895 when a team from Latrobe, Pennsylvania, played the neighboring town of Jeannette. There were some touring football teams after this, but it wasn't until 1919 when the founders of the future National Football League gathered in Canton, Ohio, to organize the sport. The great Native-American football star Jim Thorpe was elected as president of the league.

The professional game began to slowly draw people's interest. In the 1920s the great Red Grange played professional football before crowds of thousands. However, great college football teams such as Michigan, Minnesota, Notre Dame, and Army captured most of the public's attention.

In 1946 the All-America Football Conference was founded to compete with the National Football League (NFL). But it was absorbed by the NFL in 1950. Television and America's love of sports helped the NFL to flourish. Few college games were televised, but televising professional games really promoted the game.

Professional football became so profitable that the American Football League (AFL) was founded in 1960. Both leagues competed in signing new football players, and they changed their rules to allow more scoring. The NFL absorbed the AFL in 1970, and this agreement allowed for many professional football teams. They also came up with a postseason championship game, the Super Bowl. The World Football League (1974-75) and the United States Football League (1983-87) challenged the NFL, but both failed financially.

1. Remember the first professional football game you ever saw either in a stadium or on TV? What were the names of the teams? What was the final score? What was the date? Recall the sights and sounds. Can you express how you felt at the time?
2. Have you been a fan of a professional football team? What was the team? Who were your favorite players? How many years have you supported this team?
3. Did your favorite team ever play in the Super Bowl?
4. Do you have any memorabilia from your team such as pictures, programs, buttons, banners, collectors' cards, etc.
5. List the greatest professional football players and teams you have ever watched.
6. Can you name cities that have professional football teams?
7. Where do the Cowboys and 49ers live?

It happened on November 13, 1850.

Birthday of Robert Louis Stevenson

Robert Louis Stevenson was the most popular and the most successful writer of the late 1800s. People all over the world read his adventurous and romantic novels. In 1881 he made up a tale about buried treasure and pirates for his stepson. This tale expanded into *Treasure Island*, his most famous novel. This novel, which was published in 1883, describes the hair-raising adventures of the hero Jim Hawkins and the villain Long John Silver as they search for the fabulous buried treasure.

His second important novel, *The Strange Case of Dr. Jekyll and Mr. Hyde,* made him an extremely successful novelist. This book was published in 1886. It is the tale of a doctor who takes a drug that turns him into a horrible and very evil person. It is a fascinating tale of horror.

Stevenson also wrote *Kidnapped*, *The Master of Ballantrae*, plus several other novels. He also wrote many short stories, essays, travel books, and poems. The delightful *A Child's Garden of Verses*, is a collection of sweet and simple poems that are excellent examples of children's literature.

Stevenson was born on November 13, 1850, in Edinburgh, Scotland. Most of his life was spent in a battle with illness, and many of his best novels were written from a sickbed. When he was young, he suffered from a lung disease that eventually developed into tuberculosis. He always loved reading, the sea, the open air, and adventure.

He studied engineering but soon left that to study law. He passed the bar examination in 1875 but found he didn't enjoy law and never established a practice. Instead, he turned to his real love—writing.

His first book was *An Inland Voyage* (1878). After that, he had several other books published. All the time he was writing, he was also searching for a climate that would be healthful for him. He traveled to the United States and various parts of Europe searching for such a place. Finally, in 1888 he and his family sailed a yacht to the South Seas. After six years of travelling through the South Sea islands, he settled in Samoa near Apia. There he bought land, built a house, and became a planter. The Samoans loved and respected him because of his goodness and tolerance. When he died, Samoan chiefs buried him on top of Mount Vaea.

1. Stevenson is the favorite author of many—especially young people. Most of his novels are extremely adventurous. Can you recall any of his novels? What favorite scenes and characters do you remember?
2. This author is a strong example of people who are ill or handicapped most of their lives yet achieve something significant. Can you think of other examples of such people and their accomplishments?
3. When you were young, what books and authors did you enjoy reading?

Activity

Hold a "Favorite Author Day." Each person who wishes may bring one or more novels and discuss his/her favorite author and that author's work. Serve refreshments.

It happens on November 14.

Favorite Author Day

November 14 is Favorite Author Day, and this is a good time to select some books from famous American novelists to read for enjoyment. The following is a book list that has been recommended by leading scholars and avid readers for over twenty years.

1. *Moby Dick*—Herman Melville (Ahab's quest for the White Whale)
2. *Tom Sawyer*—Mark Twain (greatest boyhood novel)
3. *Look Homeward, Angel*—Thomas Wolfe (a study of values)
4. *The Grapes of Wrath*—John Steinbeck (social protest)
5. *For Whom the Bell Tolls*—Ernest Hemingway (search for a faith to believe in)
6. *This Side of Paradise*—F. Scott Fitzgerald (Jazz Age)
7. *The Sound and the Fury*—William Faulkner (Southern gothic)
8. *The Naked and the Dead*—Norman Mailer (war in the South Pacific)
9. *The Catcher in the Rye*—J.D. Salinger (sensitive novel of a young boy)
10. *To Kill a Mockingbird*—Harper Lee (racism in a small Southern town)
11. *When the Legends Die*—Hal Borland (search for identity)
12. *Exodus*—Leon Uris (Jews return to their homeland)
13. *Hawaii*—James Michener (the history of Hawaii)
14. *The Fountainhead*—Ayn Rand (search for the individual)

1. Is reading one of your favorite hobbies? What pleasure do you get out of reading?
2. What type of books do you enjoy reading? Do you like fiction, biography, or science fiction? Share with us some of the books you have enjoyed reading and tell us why.
3. Who are some of your favorite authors? Name a few and tell us what it is about certain authors that make you want to read all their books. Is it their writing style that you like or is it something else?
4. What is a book signing? Have you ever been to one? Do you have a book signed by an author? Does this make the book more valuable?

Activity

There are many novels on tape. Obtain several that present books on this list for the group's enjoyment.

It happened on November 15, 1887.

Georgia O'Keeffe Born

Georgia O'Keeffe is a well-known, modern American painter. Her paintings are simple and stark. In her paintings she enlarges and intensifies such natural items as flowers and skulls. They literally fill her canvases. She began painting these subjects in 1929. That year she moved to Taos, New Mexico. The bright sunlight and the stark simplicity of this area inspired many of her finest paintings.

She was born on November 15, 1887, in Sun Prairie, Wisconsin. Her work was first shown in 1916 at "291," a New York gallery that presented new painters who were attempting to paint new forms. She had exhibits every year from 1926 to 1946. In 1951 she exhibited at the Intimate Gallery and then later at An American Place in New York City. She also had exhibits in 1943 at the Art Institute of Chicago and the Museum of Modern Art in 1946.

She worked in advertising in 1908 and 1909 in Chicago. She was art supervisor of public schools in Amarillo, Texas, in 1916 and 1917. In 1918 she taught art in Texas. She studied at several art schools such as the Art Institute of Chicago and the Art Students' League in New York City. Her paintings include *Cow's Skull with Calico Roses*, *Black Iris*, *Lake George*, *A Cross by the Sea*, *Farmhouse Window and Door*, and *Canada*.

1. Have you ever had the opportunity to view any of Georgia O'Keeffe's paintings? If you have, what can you say about her work? Do you like it? Is it powerful? What message or messages does she attempt to present in her paintings?
2. Why does a person paint? Is it for relaxation, or does it have other value?

Activity

Find several copies of O'Keeffe's paintings and place them around the room for the group to observe and comment on. Ask an art teacher or a local artist to visit your facility to discuss the style and use of colors in his/her paintings. Then, provide different items such as flowers, rocks, pieces of wood, leaves, etc., to draw or to paint.

It happens on November 15-21.

National Geography Awareness Week

National Geography Awareness Week takes place from November 15-21. It is important that everyone be aware of and have knowledge of geography. Our world is growing and changing so rapidly that we must all have a global awareness and keep up with the name changes of cities and countries around the world.

Geography studies the earth as man's home. It points out where people live and where cities, mountains, rivers and lakes, and other geographic features are located. This subject studies why these features are there and how they are interrelated. It explains what different parts of the world are like and how they differ from each other as well as how various cultures are different and how they developed over time.

A knowledge of geography is valuable to everyone, and learning about geography begins in kindergarten and continues throughout life. The study of geography includes the ability to read maps, understand different cultures, understand directions, knowledge of climate and weather, and an understanding of geographic relationships.

Most of us gain our geographic knowledge from reading books, magazines, and newspapers; from television, motion pictures and radio; and from studying maps. Some people travel to different areas of the earth and observe. This way they learn geography firsthand.

1. What different states or countries have you visited? Which sights and cities impressed you the most?
2. Do you have a favorite state or country that you have been to several times? Did you go as a tourist or did you work and live there?
3. Can you name some or all of our fifty states? How many states have you driven through or visited? Do you know the state flower or the state bird for any of the states? Name the ones you can recall.
4. Are you good at knowing directions? Can you point out to us which direction is north, south, east, and west? Look at a map. Show and tell us what sections of the country you have lived in.
5. Is there a particular place you have always wanted to visit but have been unable to?

Activity

1. Place a large map of the United States on your bulletin board. People can write different statements on each of our states. (Example: "I've been here nine times. The Great Loon Lake was my family's favorite place to stay.")
2. Take the group on a field trip outside. Supply tablets and pens or pencils. Ask them to draw a map. Draw houses, buildings, roads, trees, fields, etc. Ask them to label each item they have drawn. Record information about that item. They are also to write down directions—north, south, etc.

November 17

American Education Week

It happens on November 15-21.

American Education Week

American Education Week was created by Presidential Proclamation 5403 in October, 1985. It is held around November 15-21 each year. Annually, it is the week preceding Thanksgiving. This week acquaints the public with the work of education and with its problems, achievements, and needs. The American Legion, the National Education Association, the National Congress of Parents and Teachers, and the U.S. Office of Education all sponsor it. American Education Week was first observed in 1921. Under the leadership of the World Federation of Education Associations, other countries have adopted the custom of observing an education week.

An American Education Week program begins with proclamations from state governors and mayors. These proclamations stress the importance of education. There are open house programs in the schools, exhibits in schools, libraries and businesses, and special programs on television. Themes such as "America Has a Good Thing Going—Its Schools" and "Invest in Learning" have been prominent.

1. Did you attend a rural, one-room school, or a multi-room school? What was the name of the school? Where was it located, and what years did you attend?
2. How many students were there in your class? How many students were in your school? Did any of your best friends go to the same school? Can you remember their names and something about each of them? Have you stayed in touch with any of them over the years?
3. What subjects did you study? Which were your favorites?
4. Did you participate in sports, band, or speech? Were you a cheerleader? Did you ever go on any memorable field trips?
5. Compare your school to today's schools.
6. Who was your favorite teacher during all your years of schooling?
7. What characteristics or qualities does a good teacher possess?
8. Would you have liked to have been a teacher? If so, what subject and grade level would you have liked to have taught?
9. What are some of the problems our schools face today? (Lack of financing, crime, drugs, etc.) How can some of these problems be solved?
10. How can we, as citizens, help our schools?

Activity

Plan a visit to a local museum that has recreated a classroom. Also, work with a retired teachers' club to help decorate your facility for American Education Week.

It happens on November 18.

Christmas Festivals

November 18 marks the beginning of three great Christmas festivals in the United States. One, called the "Festival of Trees," takes place in Davenport, Iowa, on November 18-26. There are spectacular Christmas lights all over the city, and at the River Center there are hundreds of unusual holiday creations for the home on display. This festival also offers holiday concerts, luncheons, a Holiday Hoedown, and the Festival of Trees Holiday Parade, the largest inflatable character balloon parade in the country.

Equally impressive is "La Posada de Kingsville," a celebration of lights that occurs in Kingsville, Texas. This celebration recaptures the joy and spirit of Christmas. Businesses and homes twinkle with lights from the third weekend in November through December 31. Events include a street dance, a fiesta market in the historic district, special activities for children, a lighted procession of Mary and Joseph's search for an inn, a five-kilometer jingle bell run, a nighttime parade with lighted floats and holiday music.

The third of these festivals is called "Holiday Rhapsody in Lights." This event begins on November 18 at and around Northwest Community College of Norfolk, Nebraska. There are over 300,000 holiday lights on display. Of special interest are the twelve life-sized, animated displays reminiscent of department store windows of the '40s and '50s. Scenes include the Reindeer House, Miracle on 34th Street, Candy Cane Express, Elves' Workshop, Santa's Mailroom, and others. Controlled by computer relays, there are 120 soldiers marching and 160 gingerbread men and women skating on the lake under their own London Bridge. This festival ends on January 2.

1. As a child, did you ever see any unusual Christmas parades or holiday displays of lights? Where was this? Can you recall the date?
2. When you were growing up, did you always have a Christmas tree? Can you remember what you used to decorate your tree? Did you make your own Christmas decorations? Describe some of them.
3. What were some things you had on your Christmas list? Did you ask for toys or material things, such as clothing, that you really needed? Were you ever disappointed with what you received for Christmas?
4. Compare Christmas when you were young to Christmas now. How has Christmas changed? Has it changed for the better or worse?

November 19

Great American
Trombonist and Bandleader

**Tommy Dorsey
1905-1956**

It happened on November 19, 1905.

Birthday of Tommy Dorsey

Tommy Dorsey, American trombonist and bandleader, was born in Mahoney Plains, Pennsylvania, on November 19, 1905. He and his equally famous brother Jimmy were dance band leaders and dominant figures in the golden age of "big bands" in the 1930s and 1940s.

He and Jimmy, a saxophone player and clarinetist, received their first music lessons from their father. Tommy played trumpet and other instruments in school bands. Then he learned to play the trombone and developed a technique using an unusual method of convex breathing that allowed him to maintain extremely long passages "legato" (smooth and connected).

During their teen years the Dorseys performed in parades and at local functions frequently with bands they had organized. In the late 1920s they joined the Paul Whiteman Orchestra.

Then in 1933 they formed the famous Dorsey Brothers Orchestra but parted one year later and formed separate bands. The brothers and their bands starred in their screen biography *The Fabulous Dorseys* (1947). They formed a band called "The Fabulous Dorseys." Some of Tommy Dorsey's hits include "Boogie Woogie," "I'll Never Smile Again," and "There Are Such Things." He died in 1956.

1. Have you ever owned any records the Dorseys produced? What were some of their songs?
2. Did you ever go to see and hear any of the big bands? How many people would it take to make up a band? What big bands have you seen?
3. Can you recall what type of music these big bands played? Were they tunes you could dance to? Name some of the tunes and dances.
4. Who were some of the other famous bandleaders? (Benny Goodman, Guy Lombardo, Duke Ellington, Stan Kenton, Glenn Miller, Harry James, etc.)
5. Compare a "big band" to a typical rock band of today.
    a. music
    b. number of members
    c. instruments used
    d. dress

Activity

Hold a "Dorsey Day." Play some great Dorsey tunes to dance/move to.

November 20
"Red Kettle"
Kick Off Day

It happens around November 20.

National "Red Kettle" Kick Off Day

November 20 begins National "Red Kettle" Kick Off Day for the Salvation Army's Christmas season. Thousands of volunteers will man these collection kettles to fund holiday relief effort to purchase food, clothing, and shelter for the homeless and other needy people.

The Salvation Army, an international Christian religious and charitable organization, is set up as a military system, and its people have the ranks of military officers. The Army works to present the love of God and to help the needy. Its services are offered to anyone, regardless of race, creed, sex, or age.

The Salvation Army operates hospitals, drug and alcohol rehabilitation centers, day-care centers, senior citizen residences, and boys' and girls' clubs. It also provides programs for unwed mothers, family assistance, camps, and aid to prisoners and their families.

A Methodist minister, William Booth, founded the Salvation Army in 1865 in London. He began conducting meetings to bring the message of Jesus Christ to the people in London's East End. At first, his organization was known as the Christian Mission. Later the name was changed to the Salvation Army, and it began spreading outside of Great Britain. In 1880 it was established in the United States.

Today, the Salvation Army helps people in over eighty-five countries. There are around 25,000 people serving as officers. Worldwide, there are more than fourteen thousand corps community centers. There are approximately 420,000 members in the United States. (The Salvation Army's national headquarters is located at 615 Slaters Lane, Alexandria, VA 22313.)

1. Have you ever been a Red Kettle volunteer for the Salvation Army? What does a Red Kettle volunteer do? Can you tell us what the Red kettle proceeds are used for? Have you helped the Salvation Army in other ways?
2. Does the Salvation Army operate in other countries as well? Whenever there is an act-of-nature disaster anywhere around the world, what does the Salvation Army do to help? What are some of the disasters that you can remember where the Salvation Army was there to help?
3. What are your feelings about the homeless people? Do you think the government should be doing more to help them, or should each state take care of its own? If you were visiting a large city and saw individuals or families living on the streets, what would you do? Would you just walk past them, or would you try to assist them in some way?

Activity

Use the Salvation Army in the following ways:

a. Invite their band to come and play.
b. Have the Salvation Army conduct a church service.
c. Have one of their speakers present an informational program.
d. Paint an old kettle red and contribute change. Make a presentation of this to a visiting Salvation Army member.

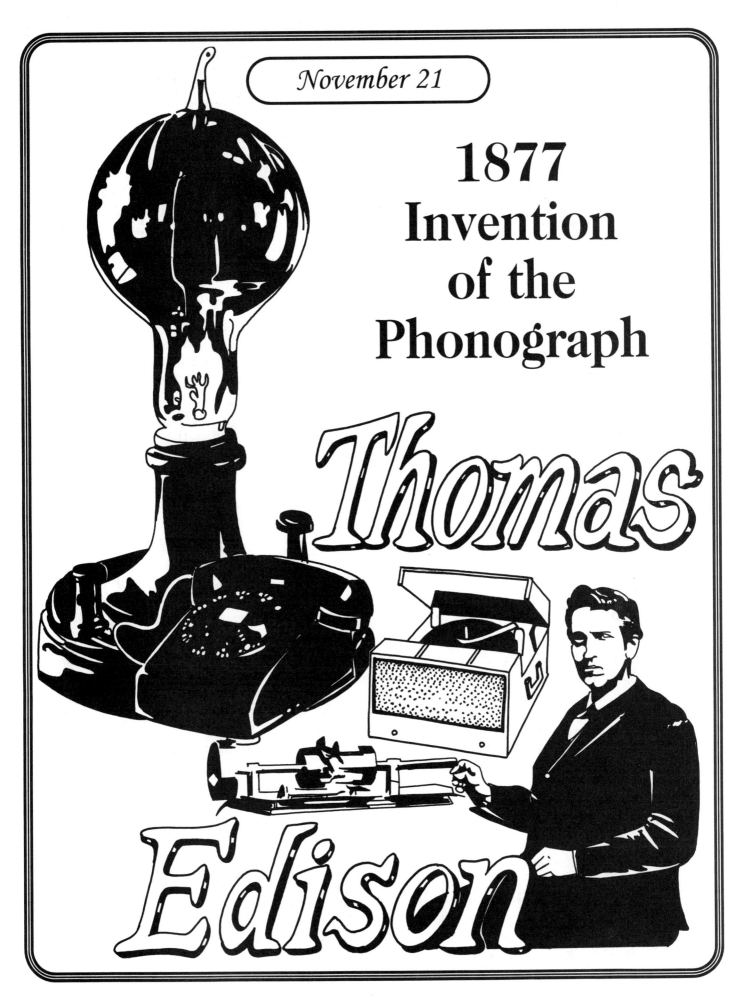

> *It happened on November 21, 1877.*

Invention of the Phonograph

Thomas Alva Edison invented the phonograph on November 21, 1877. He was probably the greatest inventor who ever lived. In sixty years he patented more than 1,100 inventions. Besides the phonograph, he invented the electric light, an electric vote-recording machine, a stencil-duplicating process and one of the first motion picture devices. He also improved other inventions. These were the telephone, the typewriter, the stock ticker, electric-powered trains, and the electric generator.

As a youngster, Thomas was extremely curious about everything. He asked questions constantly. "How do birds fly?" "Why does water put out fire?" If no one could answer his questions, he experimented to find the answers. He saw that a hen sat on her eggs and they hatched, so he got some eggs and sat on them!

His constant questions in school began to irritate his schoolmaster who said Thomas was "addled." Thomas told his mother this, and she went to school and told the schoolmaster that he was wrong about her son, and she took Thomas out of school. His formal education lasted but three months.

His mother had once been a schoolteacher, and she began teaching her son. She believed that learning should be fun. She made up games that explored the world of knowledge. Thomas was extremely happy, and he began learning so quickly that his mother was no longer able to teach him. Mrs. Edison bought him a chemistry book, and he proceeded to test every experiment in the book to see if it was correct!

Other events and jobs furthered his education. At the age of twelve he sold newspapers, candy, and sandwiches on a train. Then he was taught to be a telegrapher. Later he worked for a stock-ticker firm, and when the ticker broke down, he repaired it. He found something useful in everything he did, and he was always learning.

1. Before electricity was invented, what was used for light? Was it kerosene lamps? Can you describe what the kerosene lamps looked like? How did they work? Did their light make reading difficult?
2. Do you know what a wick is? How was it used in kerosene lamps? What did you have to do with the wick? Without it, would the lamp work?
3. Did you ever own a phonograph when you were growing up? Do you remember how old you were when you first owned one? What size records did you have to use? Was your phonograph automatic, or did you have to work it by hand? Can you recall any of the records that you had?
4. Can you name some other inventions that were patented when you were young that were of use to you? One invention was the telephone. Can you remember when your first telephone was installed? How did this change your life?
5. Think back to what inventions your mother had in her lifetime. What new inventions did you have to use that made your life easier than your mother's? Now, think about what inventions your children had or have that you didn't have when you were raising your family. Can you name some of them?

It happened on November 22, 1963.

Assassination of John F. Kennedy

John F. Kennedy, thirty-fifth President of the United States, was assassinated in Dallas, Texas, on November 22, 1963. Three other Presidents of the United States have been assassinated: Lincoln (1865), Garfield (1881), and McKinley (1901).

Assassination is usually the killing of a person who holds a position of public importance. Assassinations are performed to remove an enemy or to make money. There have been many assassinations throughout history. The Roman, Julius Caesar, was assassinated by Brutus and other Roman officials. One of the causes of World War I was the murder of Archduke Ferdinand of Austria in 1914. The Black Dragon Society in Japan committed many assassinations in the 1930s to gain control of the government for the Japanese Army. And, in 1968, Martin Luther King, Jr., was murdered in Memphis, Tennessee, while helping his fellow Negroes protest unjust treatment.

There have been other great men who have been assassinated such as Mahatma Gandhi, who was murdered in January of 1948. There have also been many attempted assassinations that have failed like the one against former President Ronald Reagan.

The word *assassination* comes from *assassins* or *hashshashin*, the plural of *hashshash*, one who smokes or chews hashish. There was a secret order of Muslims in Persia and Asia Minor who, at the time of the crusades and later, terrorized their enemies by committing secret murders while they were under the influence of hashish.

The similarities of the assassinations of Abraham Lincoln and John F. Kennedy are unusual. Present the following information for discussion.

1. Lincoln was elected President in 1860, Kennedy in 1960.
2. President Lincoln's secretary, whose name was Kennedy, advised him not to go to the theater.
3. Kennedy's secretary, whose name was Lincoln, advised him not to make the trip to Dallas.
4. Both were slain on a Friday in the presence of their wives.
5. Both were shot from behind and in the head.
6. John Wilkes Booth shot Lincoln in a theater and ran to a warehouse.
7. Lee Harvey Oswald shot Kennedy from a warehouse and ran to a theater.
8. Both assassins were killed before they could be brought to trial.
9. Both Lincoln and Kennedy were succeeded by Southern Democrats named Johnson, who held seats in the U.S. Senate.

It happened on November 23, 1859.

Birthday of Billy the Kid

Billy the Kid was the most famous of all American outlaws. His real name was Henry McCarty, and he was born on November 23, 1859, in New York City. His mother remarried, and the family moved to Silver City, New Mexico.

His mother died in 1874, and Henry became part of the wild frontier. In 1877 he shot and killed a man in a quarrel near Fort Grant, New Mexico. After the killing he became a fugitive and went to Lincoln County, New Mexico. He also changed his name to William H. Bonney.

A rancher, John H. Tunstall, gave him a job and befriended him. Tunstall was murdered in a frontier feud, the Lincoln County cattle war. The "Kid," as a member of a posse called the Regulators, helped kill the murderers. He became known as Billy the Kid, and he took a large role in the feud. He became the leader of an outlaw band that murdered and rustled cattle.

Sheriff Pat Garrett captured Billy in December of 1880. On April 9, 1881, Billy was convicted and sentenced to hang. Somehow he killed two deputies and escaped from jail. Garrett went after him and killed him in Fort Sumner, New Mexico. In his career Billy killed at least five men, but, according to legend, he killed twenty-one.

1. When you were young, did you have a favorite cowboy outlaw? Was it Billy the Kid, Jesse James, or someone else? Did you read books or see movies about this outlaw?
2. Why did people glamorize these outlaws and make them heroes? What was it about their lives and times that appealed to people?
3. Can you recall being at a movie about outlaws and other cowboys on a Saturday afternoon when you were young? Did you clap and cheer when your hero did something dramatic?
4. How were the women portrayed in these outlaw movies? Can you describe the clothing they wore?
5. Is there any difference in being a *criminal* or being an *outlaw*? Give us your opinion.

November 24

Oscar Robertson, "the Big O"

It happened on November 24, 1938.

Oscar Robertson Born

Oscar Robertson was one of basketball's all-time stars. This muscular 6'5" guard had tremendous scoring and playmaking skills. He was dubbed "the Big O" by admiring fans.

During his fifteen-year professional career with the Cincinnati Royals and Milwaukee Bucks, he scored 26,710 points. This was an average of 25.7 points per game. Along with his scoring he had 9,887 assists.

Robertson was born on November 24, 1938, in Charlotte, Tennessee. When he played high school basketball in Indianapolis, Indiana, he was picked by *Scholastic Magazine* as high school all-American.

Later, at the University of Cincinnati, he set several major college scoring records and lead the Bobcats to high national ranking. In 1960, as captain of the U.S. Olympic basketball team, he lead the team to gold-medal honors.

The Cincinnati Royals drafted him in 1961, and he was voted Rookie of the Year. Three years later he won the Most Valuable Player award.

In 1970 he was traded to Milwaukee where, along with Kareem Abdul-Jabbar, he helped lead the Bucks to their first championship. He retired from professional basketball in 1974 and was later elected to the Basketball Hall of Fame in 1979.

1. Do you like sports? Did you ever play any sports during your school years? Which sport or sports were you involved in?
2. When you were in high school or college, were there cheerleaders for the different sports? Were you ever a cheerleader? See if you can remember one of the cheers. Perhaps you could recite one for us and do a little bit of the routine.
3. Do you recall if there were marching bands to perform at the games? What instrument did you play or would have liked to play? What were the band uniforms like? Describe them.
4. Why do you think sports figures are so popular? Do you think sports heroes are given too much special attention?
5. Some other great basketball players over the years have been _____, _____, _____, _____, and _____. Who was your favorite?
6. Do you know the city where the following teams play?

   Celtics _____
   Knicks _____
   Bulls _____
   Spurs _____
   Magic _____
   Lakers _____

It happens on the fourth Thursday of November.

Thanksgiving Day

In the United States, Thanksgiving is celebrated on the fourth Thursday of November. On this day people give thanks with prayer and feasting for the blessings they have received. In our country it is usually a family day with big dinners and happy reunions. It is also a time for church service and prayer.

The first New England Thanksgiving took place in 1621 in Plymouth, Massachusetts. After a terrible winter had killed half the members of the colony, the Pilgrims celebrated their survival at an autumn harvest festival. Chief Massasoit and ninety-nine of his braves from the Wampanoag tribe were guests.

The Pilgrims provided geese, ducks, fish, johnny cake, corn meal bread, succotash, oysters, plums, and berries. The Indians brought venison, wild turkeys, and "popped corn." Everyone ate outdoors.

For many years there was no national Thanksgiving Day in the United States. Then, in 1789 President George Washington proclaimed November 26 as a day of national Thanksgiving. Some states observed a yearly Thanksgiving and others did not. By 1830 New York and other northern states had an official Thanksgiving Day. In 1855 Virginia became the first Southern state to have Thanksgiving.

Mrs. Sarah Joseph Hale, editor of *Ladies' Magazine* in Boston, worked many years to establish a national Thanksgiving Day. She wanted the fourth Thursday of November to be Thanksgiving Day. In 1863 President Lincoln proclaimed that the fourth Thursday of November would be Thanksgiving. There were some different dates for Thanksgiving over the years, but in 1841 President Franklin D. Roosevelt, once again, proclaimed the fourth Thursday as Thanksgiving Day, and we have celebrated it on that day ever since.

When we think of Thanksgiving, we think of Pilgrims, turkey, cranberries and Indian corn. The cornucopia (horn of plenty) is another Thanksgiving symbol which symbolizes the richness of the earth's bounty.

1. Compare the Pilgrims' Thanksgiving feast to a modern-day one. Discuss the circumstances the Pilgrims were in, their clothing, lodging, and food. Compare these to our own times.
2. What was the best Thanksgiving you ever had? Where were you? Who else was there? What foods were served? Why is this particular time so special?
3. Did your family have some special foods/dishes that were prepared every Thanksgiving?
4. After your family ate Thanksgiving dinner, what else did they do?
5. Some people think that Thanksgiving will eventually disappear in our country because Christmas is advertised even before Thanksgiving arrives. Do you agree or disagree?
6. What are some things you have been thankful for in life?

> *It happened on November 26, 1797.*

Sojourner Truth Born

Sojourner Truth was the name used by Isabella Baumfree, a well-known American abolitionist. She was born a slave but became a champion of her people. She was the first Negro woman to speak out against slavery. She travelled throughout New England and the Midwest championing black freedom. Her sharp wit, strong faith, and deep voice made her famous.

Baumfree was born on November 26, 1797, in Ulster County, New York. She was auctioned when she was nine and sold several more times before she became free. (New York passed a law that banned slavery in 1828.)

She worked as a servant in New York City until 1843 when she had an experience that she considered a command from God for her to preach. She began calling herself Sojourner Truth and started preaching in New York. "People show their love of God by their love and concern for other people" was her main message. Eventually she began speaking against slavery and for the rights of women. She attracted large crowds every place she spoke.

In 1864, during the Civil War, Sojourner visited President Abraham Lincoln in the White House. In Washington, D.C., she worked to improve conditions for Negroes living there. She also helped newly freed slaves and slaves who had escaped from the South to Washington. Later, she lobbied for a plan that would give ex-slaves land in the West. (This plan failed because it had no government support.) For the rest of her life, Sojourner Truth spoke out against racial injustice and for voting rights for women.

1. *Sojourner* means "to stay as a temporary resident." Do you think the name Sojourner Truth was an appropriate name for this courageous woman?
2. Why were slaves brought to America? Who brought them here? Where did the slaves come from? What are your feelings about slavery?
3. For what reason did a person buy slaves? A slave could be auctioned off several times. Do you think this was right? What do you suppose a slave would have cost? How did this problem affect our country before and after the Civil War, and how does it affect us today?
4. Are we making progress in stopping racial injustice for all Americans and in learning to be one people?

> *It happens on November 27.*

Twenty-Seven More Shopping Days

Today is November 27. There are only 27 shopping days until Christmas. Do you remember that every year starting in August you kept seeing signs and hearing commercials that told you how many shopping days were left before Christmas?

1. Do you wait until the last minute to shop for Christmas gifts?
2. What was the best Christmas gift you ever received?
3. What were some unique ways you wrapped or disguised Christmas presents?
4. Do you recall a gift you made as a child or as an adult for someone? What was it?
5. Do you think it's all right for people to shop for gifts on Sunday?
6. Do you remember going to bed when there was nothing under the tree and waking up Christmas morning and seeing all the gifts? Were you excited?
7. What is the best gift you ever gave anyone for Christmas?
8. Would you rather have a vase of flowers, homemade bread, or a book as a gift for Christmas?
9. Do you think giving money as a gift is the easy way out?
10. What was the best Christmas you ever had? Why do you recall this time as your favorite?
11. Did your children receive any unusual Christmas presents?
12. Did children receive as many presents when you were young as they do today?
13. Compare the types of gifts you received as a child to the kinds of gifts today's children receive.
14. Is there too much emphasis on money at Christmas?
15. Can you describe a typical Christmas day when you were a child?
16. Do you think people are ever too old to enjoy Christmas?
17. Did you ever buy a Christmas gift for an animal?
18. Did the wise men give the first Christmas gifts? What were these gifts?

Activity

Ask each person to pretend and make out a list of presents he/she wishes Santa Claus to bring.

It happened on November 28, 1919.

First Woman Elected to Parliament

American-born Lady Astor was a British political leader. She was born Nancy Witcher Langborne in Greenwood, Virginia, in 1879. Her first marriage to Robert Gould Shaw ended in divorce, and in 1906 she married the Englishman, Waldorf Astor. After her husband entered the House of Lords, Lady Astor was elected to his seat in the House of Commons on November 28, 1918, as a Conservative member from Plymouth.

She was the first woman to sit in British Parliament, retaining her seat until 1945. During her long career she was an advocate of temperance, an opponent of socialism, and a champion of women's and children's welfare.

During the later part of the 1930s, she was a leader of the "Clivenden set," which was accused of appeasing Germany, and she gained some bad publicity. Despite this and her discussions of irreverent subjects in Parliament, she was still regarded as one of the most colorful and wittiest people in British politics. In 1923 her book *My Two Countries* was published.

1. There have been many famous women political figures from all over the world since the time of Lady Astor. Indira Gandhi, Margaret Thatcher, and Shirley Chisholm are examples. Can you think of other female political figures?
2. Have women in the United States been too long in achieving political power? Why or why not?
3. Winston Churchill and Lady Astor didn't get along very well. Here is one of their famous exchanges. Lady Astor: "Winston, you are drunk." Winston Churchill: "Indeed, Madam, and you are ugly—but tomorrow I'll be sober."

There are endless other remarks made by and towards politicians. After Vice President Dan Quayle compared himself to Jack Kennedy, Senator Lloyd Bentsen stated, "Senator, I served with Jack Kennedy. I knew Jack Kennedy. Jack Kennedy was friend of mine. Senator, you're no Jack Kennedy." Are you able to recall any other examples such as these?

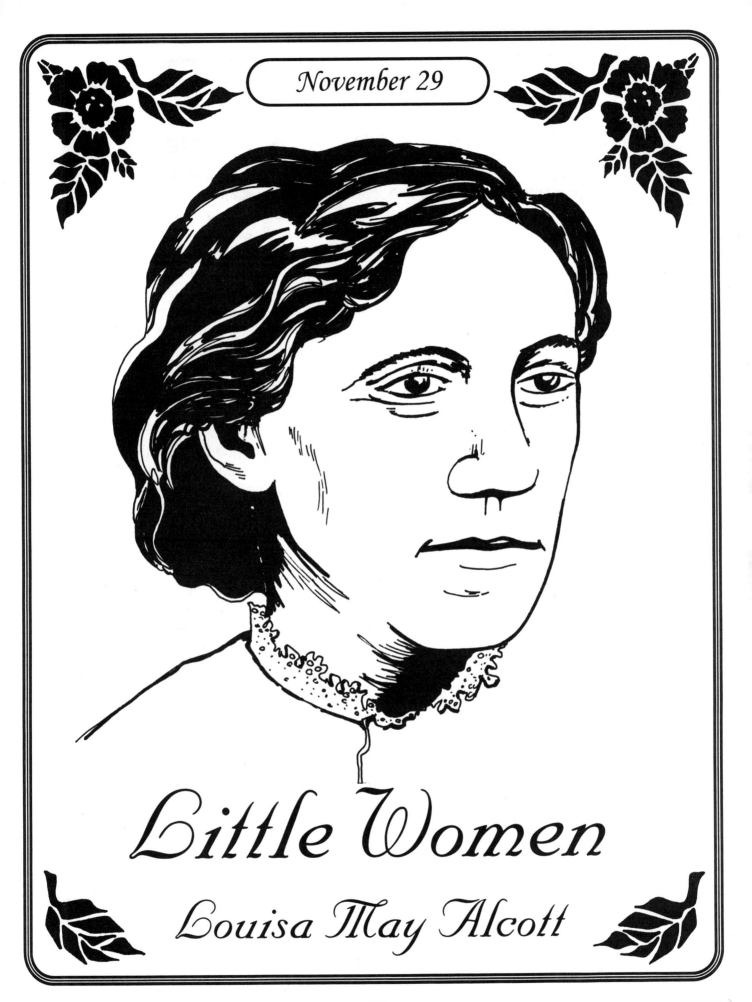

It happened on November 29, 1832.

Birthday of Louisa May Alcott

Little Women is one of the best-loved novels in our literature. It has been translated into many languages, made into movies, and has appeared on television. It was written by Louisa May Alcott and describes the experiences of Jo March and her three sisters as they grow up in a warm, family setting. The novel is really about the Alcott family, and Jo March is really Louisa.

Louisa May Alcott was born on November 29, 1832, in Germantown, Pennsylvania, to parents who were strong individuals. She was the second of four daughters. Her father was a philosopher, writer, and teacher but a poor provider for his family. In order to make money to help her family, Louisa started a small school. Later she worked in Boston. She wrote constantly. In 1864 her first novel *Moods* was published. Later she wrote *Hospital Sketches* about her experiences as a nurse during the Civil War. In 1867 a publishing house asked her to write a novel for girls. She worked hard on this novel. It was called *Little Women,* and its publication and later success brought her and her family financial security and comfort.

Little Women was so popular people wanted a sequel to it. In 1869 it was published as *Part II of Little Women*. Later she wrote *Little Men* (1871) and *Jo's Boys* (1886). Her other books are *Old-Fashioned Girl, Eight Cousins, Rose in Bloom,* and *Jack and Jill*.

1. *Little Women* is a classic novel about four sisters growing up in New England during the Civil War. It is loved by young readers as well as older ones. What is so special about this novel?
2. Do you have any brothers or sisters? How many? Were you the oldest, youngest, or in-between? It has always been said that a middle child is left out and therefore has a more difficult time growing up. Do you think this is a true statement? What is your opinion?
3. Can you describe what your family was like? Was it a warm, loving family? Tell us about your relationship with your parents, brothers, and sisters.
4. When there were problems within your family, did you all stick together to try and solve them, or did you each go your own separate ways? Can you remember a particular instance when this happened? A saying goes—"A family that prays together, stays together." Share with us your feelings about this.

Activity

There have been three movie versions of *Little Women*: Katherine Hepburn's 1933 edition, the June Allyson's 1949 version, and the 1994 picture with Winona Ryder. The last is out in video. Select one to show the group.

November 30

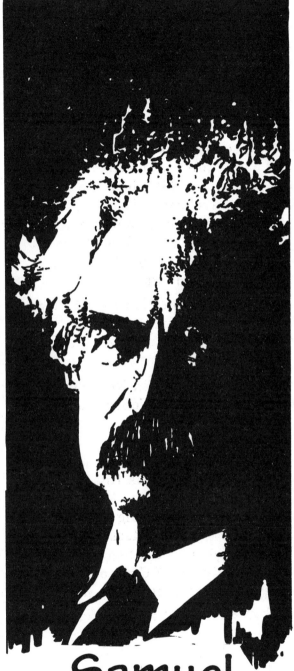

Samuel Langhorne Clemens

Tom Sawyer

The Prince and the Pauper

Huckleberry Finn

A Connecticut Yankee in King Arthur's Court

Pudd'nhead Wilson

> It happened on November 30, 1835.

Mark Twain Born

Mark Twain was the pen name of Samuel Langhorne Clemens, one of our finest American authors. He was born on November 30, 1835, in Florida, Missouri. He and his family moved to Hannibal, Missouri, in 1839. Twain grew up on the banks of the Mississippi River in this small Missouri town made famous in his book *Tom Sawyer*.

Samuel left school at the age of twelve (after his father died) and became a printer in Hannibal. In 1859 he received his pilot's license to command a steamboat. His life on the Mississippi was invaluable in his later writing. About this experience he stated, "In that brief, sharp schooling, I got personally and familiarly acquainted with about all the different types of human nature . . . ."

In July 1861 Twain moved to Nevada to search for gold. He failed to find any and began writing humorous stories of his adventures in the West. He used *Mark Twain*, a river term meaning "two fathoms," as a pen name. He received national acclaim when his story "The Celebrated Jumping Frog of Calaveras County" appeared in the New York *Saturday Press* on November 18, 1865. Twain's fame gained as he travelled abroad in the Hawaiian Islands, Europe, and the Holy Land. On each trip he sent back serious and humorous accounts of his travels. His travel book *The Innocents Abroad* was a satirical account on Americans in other countries.

Twain and his wife lived in Hartford, Connecticut, from 1871 to 1891. There he wrote his best books. These were *Tom Sawyer* (1876), *The Prince and the Pauper* (1881), *Huckleberry Finn* (1884), *A Connecticut Yankee in King Arthur's Court* (1889), and *Pudd'nhead Wilson* (1894). His precision of style, tremendous sense of humor, character development, and ability to present the way people really talked made him a giant among American writers. Ernest Hemingway said that modern American literature "begins with *Huckleberry Finn*."

1. Have you ever visited Mark Twain's boyhood home located in Hannibal, Missouri? Did you tour the cave? What did you think of it? Was it cold inside the cave? What were your thoughts as you walked through the cave? Can you imagine yourself playing in the cave as a child?
2. What books or short stories by Mark Twain have you read? Do you have particular favorites? Tell us about them.
3. *Tom Sawyer* is probably the greatest boyhood novel ever written. Are you able to recall the main characters such as Tom and Becky and favorite scenes such as the graveyard and the cave?

Activity

Read "The Celebrated Jumping Frog of Calaveras County" to the group. If they enjoy it, you might read the opening of *Tom Sawyer* where he and the new boy in town are challenging each other.